──THE── TWO MOOKS WAY

Also available
The Cotswold Way
The Dales Way
The Saxon Shore Way
The West Highland Way
The Southern Upland Way

RECREATIONAL PATH GUIDE

THE
TWO MOORS
WAY

JOHN MACADAM

Photographs by Mike Williams

Aurum Press

Ordnance Survey

Acknowledgements

I wish to thank the public library services of Devon and Cornwall, officers and rangers of Dartmoor and Exmoor National Parks, officers of Devon County Council and the district councils, English Nature, the Forestry Commission, Devon Wildlife Trust and the National Trust. Special thanks also to Steve Church and Mike Williams, to Joe Turner for creating the Two Moors Way and to those who maintain it so well. I am grateful to many others – including Sean – who provided information and good company, and to Helen and Frances for taxis, typing and walking with me. I would appreciate it if readers let me know, via Aurum Press, of any errors, my errors, which remain.

John Macadam grew up surrounded by swedes in the redland of Devon. He now lives in Cornwall, and is a member of the Outdoor Writers' Guild.

John Dehane Macadam has asserted his rights under Section 77 of the Copyright, Designs and Patents Act 1988 to be identified as the author of this work.

This guide has been compiled in accordance with the Guidelines for Writers of Path Guides published by the Outdoor Writers' Guild.

First published 1997 by Aurum Press Limited,
25 Bedford Avenue, London WC1B 3AT,
in association with the Ordnance Survey.

A catalogue record for this book is available from the British Library.

ISBN 1 85410 458 6
Book designed by Robert Updegraff
Printed and bound in Italy by Printers Trento Srl

Title page: A Bronze Age hut circle beside the 20th-century Redlake Tramway.
Front cover: The view south from Exmoor

CONTENTS

How to use this guide

This guide is in three parts:
- The introduction, historical background to the area and advice for walkers.
- The path itself, described in six chapters, with maps opposite each route description. This part of the guide also includes information on places of interest. Key sites are numbered in the text and on the maps to make it easy to follow the route description.
- The last part includes useful information such as local transport, accommodation, organizations involved with the path, and further reading.

The maps have been prepared by the Ordnance Survey® for this guide using 1:25 000 Pathfinder® or Outdoor Leisure™ maps as a base. The line of the Two Moors Way is shown in yellow, with the status of each section of the path – footpath or bridleway for example – shown in green underneath (see key on inside front cover). These rights of way markings also indicate the precise alignment of the path at the time of the original surveys, but in some cases the yellow line on these maps may show a route that is different from that shown by those older surveys, and in such cases walkers are recommended to follow the yellow route in this guide. Any parts of the path that may be difficult to follow on the ground are clearly highlighted in the route description, and important points to watch for are marked with letters in each chapter, both in the text and on the maps. *Some maps start on a right-hand page and continue on the left-hand page* – black arrows (→) *at the edge of the maps indicate the start point.* Should there have been a need to alter the route since publication of this guide for any reason, walkers are advised to follow the waymarks or signs that have been put up on site to indicate this. Parts of the Two Moors Way within the Dartmoor and Exmoor National Parks are over 'Access Land', outlined in purple on the maps. In these areas walkers do not need to follow the route shown.

Distance checklist

This list will assist you in calculating distances between places on the Two Moors Way, planning overnight stops, checking your progress or planning links to other paths. The distances are between places on the Way and do not include diversions to places off the route. At many of the locations neither accommodation nor refreshment is available and you are advised to obtain an accommodation list. If you are planning your route using the Landranger (1:50 000) maps you will be able to identify all the locations below.

Location	Approximate distance from previous location	
	miles	**km**
Ivybridge	0	0
Huntingdon Cross	9.25	14.8
Scorriton	3.0	5.0
Holne	1.0	1.5
New Bridge (National Park Information Centre)	1.0	1.5
Bel Tor car park (start of alternative routes)	2.75	4.5
Widecombe-in-the-Moor (on eastern route)	3.5	5.5
Lettaford (on eastern route)	5.5	8.8
Frenchbeer	2.5	4.0
Chagford Bridge (for Chagford, and Taw-Teign Link)	2.5	4.0
Drewsteignton	4.5	7.0
Hittisleigh Church	2.5	4.0
Prestons (for Colebrooke)	4.25	6.8
Morchard Road (for the 'Tarka Line')	5.0	8.2
Morchard Bishop	2.5	4.0
Washford Pyne	5.25	8.5
Witheridge	2.0	3.0
Bradford Mill	2.0	3.0
Knowstone	5.25	8.5
Yeo Mill	2.5	4.0
West Anstey	1.25	2.0
Hawkridge (for the Exe Valley Path)	2.75	4.5
Tarr Steps	2.0	3.0
Withypool	4.0	6.5
Ford near Cow Castle (start of alternative routes)	3.75	6.0
Simonsbath (on eastern route)	2.25	3.7
Exe Head (routes, and Tarka Trail, join)	2.5	4.0
Hoar Oak Tree	1.0	1.8
Cheriton	2.5	4.0
Lynmouth	3.0	5.0

KEY MAP

— Two Moors Way

▶2 Chapter start point

0 km   10   20

0 miles   10

Porthcawl

BRISTOL

Lundy

Ilfracombe

Lynton

A39

A3123

A361

A399

Exmoor

▶6

Barnstaple
or
Bideford Bay

Barnstaple

Hartland Point

R Taw

South
Molton

A361

▶5

Bideford

Great Torrington

A39

R Torridge

A388

A386

A377

Tiver

Bude

Holsworthy

A3072

A3072

Copplestone
(with Railway Sta)

▶4

Cred

R Tamar

A3079

Okehampton

A30

Exeter

Launceston

A395

A386

▶3

Camelford

A30

Dartmoor

A382

A38

Wadebridge

A388

Tavistock

Newton
Abbot

A389

A390

A386

▶2

Bodmin

A38

Liskeard

A30

Saltash

Plymouth

Buckfastleigh

A385

Totnes

A3022

Lostwithiel

A391

Looe

A387

Torpoint

A38

Ivybridge
(with Railway Sta)

A381

Fowey

St
Austell

A390

Whitsand
Bay

A379

Kingsbridge

Start

Bigbury
Bay

A379

Start

Salcombe

INTRODUCTION

WALKING THE TWO MOORS WAY

The Two Moors Way is a walk of great contrasts, from rolling, high moorland broken by steep-sided granite tors to lowland valleys with sluggish, willow-choked streams. Between the wilderness of Dartmoor and Exmoor, the two moors, lies central Devon, rich farm-land with red and brown soils, small villages, thatched cottages and silent, square-towered churches. Although farming and tourism are the main occupations nowadays, the route takes you past signs of earlier industries, mining for tin and iron, china clay pits and quarries. On the moorland the time span of visible human endeavour expands dramatically with Iron Age and Bronze Age settlements high on bracken- and heather-covered hillsides, suggesting former climates far more amenable to cultivation.

On a far shorter time scale, the weather on the moors can change with dramatic speed, even in summer, and walkers must be prepared to use a compass to navigate in zero visibility, indeed in some condi-tions it is folly even to start walking on the moor. After rain some of the lowland stretches become very muddy – a mere inconvenience – but the really marshy areas now have boardwalks, probably as much to protect the orchids as to help walkers.

In fine weather on the moors please remember that most of the unenclosed land is 'Access Land', edged with purple on the maps, where you are free to roam where you will. Indeed, walkers are encouraged to do so in preference to eroding a single track into a deep scar on the land. Where you are following a narrow track you are asked to walk in single file rather than widen the damage into a broad scar. Most of the problems of man-made erosion on the route are caused by horse-riders and car-borne day-trippers who walk from the roadside car park to the nearest tor. You may find the route has changed from that shown on the maps in which case do follow the waymarks. On moorland Dartmoor waymarks are intentionally scarce, but the National Park Authority may well have decided that a track has become over-used and needs repairing, or just time to recover. Away from the moors, route changes usually happen because new access agreements and cleared rights of way allow yet another stretch of tarmac to be bypassed. The Two Moors Way has indeed been modified many times since it was inaugurated in 1976. In places alternative routes exist and the total length is about 89 miles (143 km).

This guide has been written from south to north because it makes following the maps easier and also because the prevailing wind is south-west. The route has been divided into six sections of between 12½ and 19 miles (20 to 30.3 km) with villages at each end. Places to stay are spread along the route, both in villages and in scattered farms, so armed with an accommodation list you can plan your walks to suit yourself. Some people rush the walk in a long weekend, some even run, but most travel more slowly, enjoying the rich variety of wildlife, the archaeology, the villages and yes, the cream teas.

When you complete the Two Moors Way you can add your name to the many others in the books kept in the visitor centres in Lynmouth and Ivybridge. In 1976 the inauguration party clattered rapidly between the four dated granite waymarks by helicopter: if you are fortunate enough to see the sun setting over the steep North Devon coast as you approach Lynmouth your average speed may drop towards that of the snail, and you may choose to dawdle long after office hours to watch the lights come on in the village far below, rather than hurry down to bother with the trivia of adding your name to a book. Some people walk the Two Moors Way to add another tick to their list of achievements, others to enjoy a part of the world where humans still tread fairly lightly on the face of the Earth, and where, if you travel quietly and with your eyes and ears open, you will see and hear a wealth of wildlife: buzzards, curlew, woodpeckers, dippers, deer, hares and much, much more.

DARTMOOR

Dartmoor is often called a wilderness, which is ironic as the signs of man's activities over nearly five thousand years are everywhere to be seen, especially before the thick blanket of bracken spreads over much of the slopes. The geological history of Dartmoor goes back far further of course to the origin of the granite, around 285 million years ago, which was almost the last act in the plate movements that welded the crumpled rocks of South Devon and Cornwall onto the rest of Britain. The granite was intruded as a very hot liquid, baking

Dartmoor ponies are far removed from their solid, hardy ancestors. Though much loved by tourists, they are not a commercial proposition for their owners.

the rocks around and above it. The liquid cooled and crystallized, forming the typical Dartmoor granite with large conspicuous crystals of white feldspar separated by smaller crystals of white feldspar, grey quartz and shiny mica. Liquids circulated through cracks in the granite and some carried tin in solution: this was deposited in veins as tin oxide, the dark brown mineral cassiterite. The veins usually also have quartz and tourmaline, a black mineral, but many veins carry just the last two and no tin and so are valueless. In some areas the circulating water helped to rot the feldspar to form kaolin, china clay. Deep weathering in the warm and humid Tertiary Period, about 50 million years ago, rotted the granite leaving more-resistant areas less affected, and when later the soils were stripped away these areas formed the tors. Possibly much of this erosion occurred in the summers in the Ice Ages when Dartmoor was tundra, like parts of Alaska and Siberia today. Water would have also got into the joints in the rock and frozen, breaking up the rounded tors into more angular pieces that form the clitter, the natural piles of waste rock around many tors and on hillsides.

The vegetation on the moor when man first started to settle was probably oak woodland, leading into birch scrubland with possibly heath on the highest ground. Clearance of the woodland for growing crops and for pasture, and a cooling climate, led to the formation of bog and increasingly poor soils, leading in time to the abandonment of much of the higher ground. But this desertion has left a wealth of archaeological remains: the stone rows and circles, hut circles and enclosures, and the reaves. The latter – parallel low banks running for miles across the moor and dividing up the land – are evidence of a highly organized society when they were made.

Later exploitation of the moor for grazing, for alluvial mining for tin, quarrying granite and digging china clay must have destroyed many prehistoric remains but has also added its own record to the face of the moor. In medieval times the tinners were so important that they had their own stannary parliament, and their own prison at Lydford, and could look for tin wherever they wished. The earliest workings were in the valley bottoms where streams were diverted to wash away the lighter rock, and in the process the characteristic hummocky surface was produced. Later miners worked the lodes forming gulleys on the hillsides, and the most recent miners dug shafts to get at the ore underground. The miners paid their dues to the crown and after the Duchy of Cornwall was set up for the monarch's eldest son in 1337 he received the money.

The farmers on and around the moor developed their own style of dwelling, the longhouse. These were built from the 13th to the 17th century and although known from elsewhere, exceptional numbers are preserved and still lived in on the eastern side of Dartmoor. Longhouses had accommodation for humans in one half, and animals in the other, separated by a cross-passage that initially served both. The fireplace was in the middle to warm both halves and the houses were built so the animals' half (the shippon) drained through a hole in the wall. Usually, the houses are built down the slope of the hill, sometimes with a prominent dung hole in the lower end wall. Many other buildings, also made from granite, had different functions on the farm. The farmers had their own enclosed land as well as commoners' rights, such as grazing and cutting peat, on the common land. They also had the right to enclose a certain amount of extra land to form 'newtakes'.

At various times entrepreneurs have tried, and failed, to turn Dartmoor into fruitful fields of corn. In the 19th century Sir Thomas

Tyrwhitt founded Prince's Town, now Princetown, developed quarries and built the prison to hold the French and American prisoners-of-war then kept in rotting hulks at Plymouth. His ventures largely failed and Princetown only survives in its isolated location because the prison re-opened to hold civilians.

The isolation and wilderness of the moor has long been seen as ideal for military training, but today the area used is restricted to the northern part of the moor and is remote from the route of the Two Moors Way.

By Victorian times there was a counter-pressure to preserve the way of life and the archaeology of Dartmoor from those who sought to maximize the commercial exploitation of the moor, and in 1883 the Dartmoor Preservation Association was founded. By the 1950s national legislation had caught up with the Victorian mood for conservation of wild places, and National Parks were designated. Dartmoor qualified for National Park status because of the large expanse of wild country (even if it was not strictly wilderness), the wealth of archaeological remains, and the interest of the wildlife, which includes many species at the edge of their range. Northern species live on Dartmoor because it is an upland, and southern and south-western species survive because the upland is so far south.

Under the Environment Act 1995 all the National Park Authorities have two equal purposes. One is 'conserving and enhancing the natural beauty, wildlife and cultural heritage of the area', while the other is 'promoting opportunities for the understanding and enjoyment of the area's special qualities by the public'. The longer-term vision is crucial but it should not disadvantage present-day generations. The beauty of the moor is maintained by having a viable economy and on Dartmoor this is contributed to by farming, tourism, forestry, the military, quarrying and other activities. The Authority also encourages debate about how a viable and sustainable economy might be achieved. While the Authority is a grant-making body and can encourage sustainable developments, for example green tourism and the production of high-value farm products, inappropriate exploitation of the moor, such as the building of roads and reservoirs, and reafforestation with conifers, would be resisted. In 1994 Dartmoor was designated as an Environmentally Sensitive Area (ESA), which means that farmers can be paid by the Ministry of Agriculture, Fisheries and Food (MAFF), to practise low-impact farming. For example, farmers within the scheme are paid to have stocking levels such that the archaeological and cultural heritage is preserved and the wildlife value of the moor is enhanced.

BETWEEN THE MOORS

Central Devon is a land of gently undulating fields, small villages and scattered farms. The soil is mostly grey or brown, and often clayey but, unlike Dartmoor, rock very rarely shows at the surface. Where it does it is usually the sandstones and shales that continue westward to form the superb cliffs of folded strata to be seen on the coast from Tintagel in North Cornwall to Braunton in North Devon. Around Crediton a tongue of red land extends westwards, developed on sediments deposited in valleys in the ancient mountain chain. These sediments are interpreted as evidence of sand dunes, flash floods and great alluvial plains, and can be seen from the train along the coast between Exeter and Teignmouth. The cutting at the end of the M5 exposes everything except the desert sand dunes, which are now under the daffodils at the Junction 30 roundabout. There were also outpourings of lava, which is usually easy to recognize when used in buildings as it is red with blobs or streaks of white. These blobs are the infilled gas bubbles from the original eruption.

Apart from the churches where stone was used, most of the buildings are made of cob, the traditional building material in the county from at least the 13th century to about 1850. Cob is made of a damp mix of earth and chopped straw and the composition and colour depends on the colour and texture of the local soil. So long as it is kept dry, usually by a hat of thatch, a coat of limewash, and its feet on a base of pebbles or rubble, cob lasts well and the usual 3-foot thick wall has more than adequate strength for domestic architecture. Cob walls have a high thermal mass and so keep a house cool in summer, and warm in winter. After the oil crisis in the early 1970s Devon County Council experimented with fibreglass-coated cob. The main problem with cob is that it is difficult to repair as the material shrinks as it dries, but researchers at the Centre for Earthen Architecture at Plymouth University are working on the problem and aim to keep the cob housing stock in Devon good for a few more hundred years. In pre-conservation days, cob buildings that were no longer needed were knocked down and the cob recycled.

Most place names in Devon are of Saxon origin. Devonshire is itself recorded in the Anglo-Saxon Chronicle under the year 851 when 'the men of Defenascir fought the heathen army at Wicganbeorg and after making great slaughter obtained the victory'. But generally the Saxon take-over in the 7th and 8th centuries was more colonization than invasion. The existing Celtic population had been sparse, with woodland and damp waste predominating. Scattered farms developed as

The 'redland' of Devon is famous for its swedes, though here at Pashcoe Farm the crop is maize for silage.

this was brought into cultivation. Most of the grazing land up to the enclosures of the mid 18th century would have looked very similar to the present-day Knowstone Moor, and this would have been grazed by hardy native sheep and cattle. Nowadays most of the farms run Friesian dairy herds, with the arable land concentrated on the 'redland' where swedes are the traditional crop. Two other traditional products of Devon farms are clotted cream and cider, and many still have their cider-making equipment slowly crumbling away in barns. Troughs, crushing wheels and the bases of the later mechanical presses are rescued as desirable garden ornaments, while most of the mass-produced fizzy product now on sale bears little resemblance to cider that you can still buy from some farms and from barrels in a few pubs. In the 19th century granite crushing wheels were superseded by mechanical crushers consisting of rotating cogged cylinders driven by a horse-engine. The pulp is wrapped in hessian or straw, this 'cheese' pressed and the juice run into oak barrels and fermented. A large space was needed to store the cider for the following year: on the Rolle estate in East Devon labourers were paid two quarts a day in the late 19th century as part of their wages and even in the mid 1960s some farmers took flagons of their cider, their Ferguson tractors and their casual labour (like me) haymaking and harvesting. Most of the orchards with cider apples have been grubbed up but grants are available through Devon's Orchards Project to plant the traditional mix of varieties to provide adequate sugars and tannins. At present apple concentrate is imported from Normandy, and apples from Hereford for the cider factories in central Devon, but the new trees will soon bear fruit and Devon cider will again be made mostly from local apples, such as Devonshire Quarrendon, Plympton Pippin, Devonshire Crimson Queen, Pigsnout, Star of Devon, and Slack Ma Girdle. Maybe some farmers will even brave the regulations and get their crushers and their presses working again, though the thought of sterilizing the juice and then needing to add fermenting agents will stick in many a throat!

EXMOOR

Exmoor's high plateau cut by steep-sided valleys is both characteristic of and quite different from that of the other moors in the southwest that have developed on granite. But the clay soils on the slate under Exmoor will not let the rain through and so Exmoor too has its blanket bogs on the plateau. The northern part of the moor is on sandstone with free draining soils.

Before the arrival of humans, Exmoor was mostly woodland but by the end of prehistoric times much had been cleared. The Normans made the area the Forest of Exmoor – forest in this sense meaning that it was a royal hunting preserve. Red deer were the main quarry and though the villagers living around the forest had various rights the penalties under forest law for stealing one of the King's deer were severe. The moorland was also home to the hardy native ponies.

During the Commonwealth Crown lands were sold off and James Boevey bought the forest of Exmoor only to lose it when the monarchy was restored. The Crown made little money out of Exmoor and had little use of so distant and dubious a pleasure ground, and so in 1818 the forest was put up for enclosure, allotment and sale by tender. John Knight, a Midlands iron-master, acquired three-quarters of the land, and much of what we see today stems from his vision. He and his son Frederic imported miners from Cornwall, shepherds and sheep from the north, built miles of walls and beech hedges, ploughed deep to break up the iron pan that impeded drainage, limed the soil and, in general, changed totally the look of Exmoor. In the process much of the evidence of prehistoric archaeology was destroyed.

When National Parks were set up, Exmoor was included on the strength of the heather and grass moorland and the fact that many plants and animals were on the edge of their range. But nationally

The Mason Arms in Knowstone.

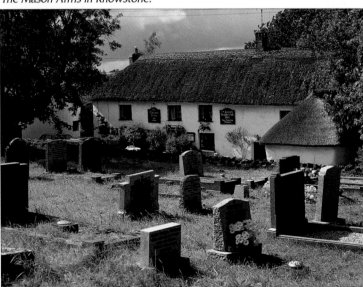

farmers were still being encouraged to increase production and grassland was still being ploughed up, and so the aims of the embryonic park were often in conflict with the aims of the farmers. To a lesser extent the same is still true, though further designation as an ESA means that farmers can be compensated for having less impact on the environment. The National Park Authority has also bought land when it could and now owns nearly 8 per cent of the National Park. In addition the National Trust owns about 10 per cent of the National Park, and in total 66 per cent of the eligible land is now managed according to ESA guidelines.

Today the National Park Authority is working to enhance the landscape by restoring a range of lost habitats, a very different vision to John Knight's, as well as ensuring that those who live on Exmoor have a livelihood. Many of the cottages in the villages are second homes that contribute little to the local economy, which relies increasingly on tourism, not farming, even if the ratio of sheep to humans is fifty to one! Over half the income of the area is now thought to be derived from tourism and visitors increasingly come for the peace of the ' barren morisch ground' that Leland wrote about in 1540, and of course there lies another problem. So far this small national park has not suffered from being loved to death, and erosion by humans and problems caused by vehicles are as yet very localized.

Topical Reading

You will have to spend far more time reading than walking if you wish to read all the fiction in print that is set on the two moors. Most famous must be Conan Doyle's *Hound of the Baskervilles*, published in instalments in 1901–2 and eminently suitable reading in a lonely, mist-shrouded tent. With luck you will only meet, in daylight, an over-enthusiastic sheepdog rather than a 'huge creature, luminous, ghastly and spectral'. The *Hound*, narrated by Dr Watson, was so popular that Conan Doyle resurrected Sherlock Holmes after apparently disposing of his creation in a watery embrace with the evil Professor Moriarty below the Reichenbach Falls in 1891. Any 'footprints of a gigantic hound' that you see will probably be those of someone's pet walking the Two Moors Way: the 'Beasts' that are regularly reported to hunt the moors today are usually described as feline ... and will leave distinctive pugmarks around your tent.

Quite different stories of Dartmoor life were written by the prolific, but now largely forgotten, Eden Phillpotts. Only *Widecombe Fair* is still in print. R.D. Blackmore's classic romance set on Exmoor, *Lorna*

Doone, has had far greater success since it was published in 1869, selling innumerable copies with several paperback editions now available, and has even become a set book in schools. And while Conan Doyle's story had as its core the tales of 'wisht' hounds, Blackmore's is based on the folk memory of a gang that terrorized Exmoor from its base in the Badgworthy area in the 17th century.

In complete contrast is Henry Williamson's *Tarka the Otter*, his most famous tale of wildlife. Although most of the action is in 'the country of the Two Rivers', the Taw and the Torridge, Tarka also travels over The Chains and down the Hoar Oak Water to Lynmouth, pursued by hounds. The end is a final epic struggle between Tarka and Deadlock, a quadrupedal version of Holmes's fight with Moriarty. Unlike Holmes, Tarka was never resurrected.

WALKING IN DEVON

Devon County Council and its partners are developing a network of interconnecting paths, an off-road highway for pedestrians. Already from the Two Moors Way you can join the coast path, either in North Devon at Lynmouth or in South Devon via a branch of the Erme-Plym Trail. But also from Hawkridge you can take the Exe Valley Path down river to the mouth of the Exe, where the ferry will take you to Exmouth for a great circular walk in East Devon following the coast path east then the East Devon Way back to the Exe. Some miles south-west down the coast the Templer Way will take you inland from Teignmouth beside the estuary, along a canal and up the old tramway to the quarries at Haytor, from where it is a short walk through Widecombe-in-the-moor back to the Two Moors Way. If, instead of taking the Templer Way, you had carried on walking to Plymouth and joined the Plym Valley Path to the West Devon Way this would in turn lead to the Tarka Trail, a 180-mile (290-km) figure-of-eight route through the northern half of Devon. The Tarka Trail includes parts of the South West Coast Path and does itself join the Two Moors Way on Exmoor.

More links are being added to the network so that Devon's ideal green tourists, with limitless time and a certain amount of money, will be perpetually walking the county's paths, never quite finishing the whole network. Just occasionally these paragons of sustainment will need to replace their boots. Finally, they and their boots will be recycled as fine humus for the organic, locally grown lettuce served in the establishments which have signed up to Devon's Green Charter for tourist operators.

Weather

Dartmoor and Exmoor may be in the south of England, and their maximum height may be only just over 2,000 feet (610 metres) but assuming the weather in summer will be sunny with a nice breeze is a folly many regret. The weather can indeed be hot and sunny and all the tourist board photographs and holiday programmes do not lie, but for two days in May 1996 the TV news was filled with footage of hundreds of school children and students in 'atrocious conditions' on Dartmoor. They were on the annual Ten Tors walk organized very thoroughly by the Army. In 1996 the event was curtailed and everyone taken off the moor very efficiently; a few cases of mild hypothermia were dealt with. For a few days people equated Dartmoor with very nasty conditions, but the tourist images quickly make people forget, and the message that the weather can, and does change, very quickly, must be heeded by walkers. Within an hour the weather can change from a lovely hot sunny day, with views for miles, to a chilling mist in which a party needs to keep in physical contact to avoid being separated, and navigation has to be by compass. In summer downpours, wind-driven rain and hail are quite common.

Remember that the conditions anywhere in Britain can be very different at the end of a day's walk to the weather when you started!

The other great variable on the moors is the going underfoot, which may be firm in one spot yet impassable bog a few feet away. Heavy rain may also turn small streams into torrents that necessitate diversions.

The implications for walkers on the Two Moors Way are fourfold: to be properly equipped, to be able to use the equipment, to plan the route ahead and to know when to turn back or even not to start.

Equipment

Equipment for the outdoors can cost a great deal of money and the critical questions are whether the gear is adequate for its intended use, and, most importantly, whether it will continue to be adequate. Far too much expensive gear fails after a few miles or a few years. That is no problem if you wish to pose on a short walk to the post box but it could be life-threatening on Dartmoor. Most gear tests published in magazines are carried out very quickly; but occasionally results of long-term tests are published that indicate which waterproofing systems keep on working (reproofable garments are best) and which manufacturers usually produce good equipment. That said, for the Two Moors Way you need a waterproof outer layer and waterproof boots (fabric are adequate). You also need to carry layers of clothing that you can put on or remove as necessary. Polycotton trousers are preferable to jeans, which become sodden and stiff and take much heat from your body as they dry, increasing the risk of hypothermia. You should also carry a compass, a whistle, a brightly coloured survival bag, a small first-aid kit, water and some energy-giving food.

VERY BASIC NAVIGATION

Most walkers carry Silva-type compasses that have a rectangular baseplate. The baseplate has a direction-of-travel arrow.

All the maps in this book observe the convention that north is at the top of the page.

Orientating the map is done in three stages. First, you rotate the north on the compass housing so that it corresponds to the direction-of-travel arrow. Second, you need to place the compass on the flat map with the direction-of-arrow travel pointing north (i.e. up the page along a vertical grid line). Next, you turn the map until the red end of the needle points to north on the compass housing. The position of features on the ground should just about correspond with their position on the map.

To use the compass to walk along the route shown on the map involves two extra steps. The first is to place the edge of the compass baseplate along the intended route, with the direction-of-travel arrow pointing in the direction you wish to go. Now turn the housing so that north points to north on the map. To walk the route you hold the compass level, keep the red end of the compass needle over the arrow in the housing, and go in the direction-of-travel arrow.

To measure distances on the map remember that the blue grid lines are 1 km apart. All the route maps are at a scale of 1:25 000 so 1 centimetre on the map is equivalent to 250 metres on the ground, which you can convert into paces. The final thing to remember when planning your route is Naismith's rule, which is that you should allow 15 minutes for each kilometre on flat ground plus 4 minutes for every 30 metres of height gained. You need to allow extra time for groups, carrying loads, climbing over stiles and opening and closing gates, and for tiredness.

You should always know where you have got to on the map, and if conditions are obviously deteriorating this is doubly important.

The very basic instructions above are designed to help people get out of difficulties. Ignoring $3\frac{1}{2}$ degrees of magnetic variation should not cause further problems. There are many good texts on map-reading and navigation, and these instructions are not meant to be a substitute for being prepared!

SAFETY

If you need to summon help the accepted distress signal is six long blasts on the whistle followed by silence for one minute.

If you need the help of the rescue teams you must contact them through the police. The teams on Dartmoor and Exmoor are all volunteers, and spend time training others, practising rescues and occasionally being called out. They also spend time rattling tins for funds to supplement the small grants they receive; you would like to help, their addresses are on pp.139–40 in the Useful Information section.

One particular hazard on the moors is ticks. These can vary in size from not much bigger than a pin head to a coffee bean. You have the highest risk of picking one up if you walk through bracken, so wearing trousers tucked into socks or inside gaiters will stop them reaching your skin. You can remove ticks by holding their heads with tweezers or tissue paper and twisting anti-clockwise. A few ticks carry Lyme disease, which can be fatal but is easily cured by antibiotics. The symptoms are varied and can take time to develop but include a red blotch around the bite and flu-like symptoms, including aching joints. If any of these develop see your doctor.

Another hazard on the moors is the bogs. In the unlikely event that your exploration of the access land takes you into one unwittingly, the critical action is to lower your pressure on the surface by spreading your weight. You can do this by slithering out on your stomach, using your rucksack and spare clothing to further spread the load.

It has also been known for the ponies on the moors to be a hazard to walkers as just occasionally they kick or bite if you try to feed them. Usually humans are a danger to the ponies because the ponies stray onto the roads after 'treats'. On Dartmoor there is now a 40 mph speed limit for vehicles, which is reducing casualties, and for many years there has been a well-advertised bye-law prohibiting visitors feeding any livestock, which obviously includes ponies.

The last point concerns dogs. Cows are sometimes aggressive towards dogs so if you are walking through a field of cows that approach you, drop the lead to let the dog escape. If young cattle follow you, let the dog go. If you are walking through a field of sheep keep your dog on a lead, and from March to the end of June you must keep your dog on the lead on the moor for the safety of lambs, ewes and nesting birds.

The compact village of Drewsteignton lies just inside Dartmoor National Park.

THE
TWO MOORS
WAY

1 IVYBRIDGE TO HOLNE

via Scorriton   *13.25 miles (21.3 km)*

Most of this section is on the moor over 'access land' where you are free to roam, so you can either use the route shown on the map, which follows a tramway, or you can make your own route. In poor visibility you should follow the tramway. There are two alternative routes near the end of the section. The beginning and end of the section are on roads and rights of way.

The Two Moors Way starts from the Tourist Information Centre (TIC) **A** beside the River Erme in Ivybridge. Nearby is the South Dartmoor Leisure Centre with indoor and outdoor swimming pools, a facility that might be very welcome to tired walkers who have just finished the 100 miles (161 km) from Lynmouth! In the town there is a wide range of shops, banks, a post office and an outdoor gear shop. In 1996 the TIC was open all year, and could provide a mass of information, including an accommodation list for the Way, though there was surprisingly little in the way of bed and breakfast accommodation in the town. You should be able to reach Ivybridge by train and bus with few problems, but you might choose to walk from the South Devon coast thus extending the Two Moors Way into a coast-to-coast walk. From the TIC you can walk down river along the Erme Valley Trail, waymarked with a waterwheel sign, to Ermington and Sequer's Bridge, but here, before you reach the sea, you will need to leave the river and walk along roads. A different route to the coast would be to take the Erme-Plym Trail, which has links to Wembury and Bovisand on the South West Coast Path, Britain's longest National Trail at some 600 miles (966 km), and which the Two Moors Way reaches at Lynmouth in North Devon.

But this book is about the Two Moors Way so however you have reached Ivybridge you need to walk up the riverside path from the TIC between two old walls made of various local rocks. Ivybridge is just to the south of the Dartmoor granite, and in the bed of the River Erme is an amazing variety of granites and the rocks baked by the hot granite around 285 million years ago. A good selection of these rocks was used in these walls, a model of local distinctiveness.

The path opens out into Costly Street and then you cross the old main road onto Harford Road. Beside a small car park is a large water turbine **1**. Ivybridge grew around the Ivy Bridge, just upstream, which

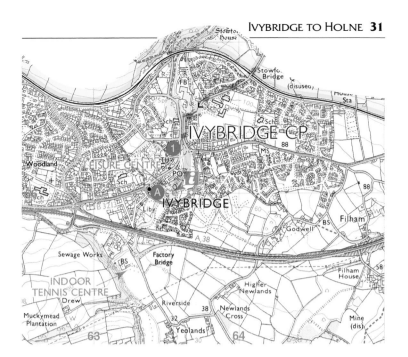

You can extend the Two Moors Way from Dartmoor south to the sea.

is mentioned in a document dated 1280. It was important enough to be shown on Speed's map of 1610, and in the late 1700s was widened to carry the coaches on the Exeter to Plymouth turnpike, when the Plymouth to London run took almost two days. If you look at the underside of the present bridge the widening is obvious, but the alteration did little for the problem of the sharp turn coaches had to make on each side of the bridge. Ivybridge was also on the route of the South Devon Railway, later the Great Western Railway (GWR), originally designed by Isambard Kingdom Brunel as a single-track, broadgauge atmospheric railway. Broad gauge meant 7ft ¼in: Britain's standard gauge of 4ft 8½in was referred to dismissively by GWR as narrow gauge! Wooden trestles on granite piers carried the sinuous route over the Erme but that bridge was replaced in 1893 by the present granite and brick structure. Granite of adequate strength was quarried only a mile away on the southern slopes of Western Beacon.

Further up the road is Stowford Paper Mills **2**, in existence since 1787, though the present factory dates from 1862 and was the cause of the main growth of the town. The River Erme provided clear water and power for these mills and was also used to power mills to grind corn for flour or grist (stock feed), and to full cloth. Further upstream, above Harford, the river was used to work the 'stamps' (rock crushers) and bellows in the 'blowing houses' used by medieval tin smelters. The fulling (or tucking) mill cleaned, thickened and flattened the cloth woven from the wool of the local sheep, probably using stale urine as a scouring agent since no fuller's earth is found in Devon. The rest of the process involved paddles and hammers to thicken and shape the cloth, which was then stretched out on racks to dry.

At the cross-road is the first granite Two Moors Way marker **B**, commemorating the inauguration of the route in 1976. The London to Penzance mainline marks the edge of the Dartmoor National Park (DNP) here so the DNP sign, with its frisky Dartmoor pony, is on the bridge. Walkers who have come by train may choose to follow the contours from the station **C** by using the new pedestrian and cycle track on the south side of the line, joining the route here, rather than walking down one road into Ivybridge then back up another: there are plenty more enjoyable climbs to come! And though alighting from a train at Ivybridge was a possibility from 1848 to 1959, it has taken a grant from the European Union's Regional Development Fund to build a new station.

Over the bridge at Stowford Farm **D** you need to turn right along the bridlepath and go through a final gate **E** onto open moor, passing the last 'MW' sign for several miles. The bridlepath was formerly used as a drove road along which cattle were driven to summer grazing on the moor.

You are now on access land, which means you can walk or run or jog where you like, though of course you are expected to observe the Country Code, which you will find at the back of this book. If you are backpacking there are also bye-laws you should observe; guidance on camping is in the Useful Information section on p.138 You have the right to roam on some of the access land by virtue of the Dartmoor Commons Act 1985, and on other parts because the National Park Authority has entered into an access agreement with the landowner. Throughout the National Park you should keep all dogs on the lead during the lambing and nesting season from March to the end of June.

You can of course follow the route shown on the map and described below. If visibility is poor this route is very easy to follow as it uses a disused tramway. It is also an easy route to retreat to if conditions deteriorate. The tramway runs broadly north–south so unless your use of the access land has taken you north of where the Way turns east all you need to do is to walk either west or east to find the tramway. This, I hope, reinforces the point made in the Introduction that you should always know where you are on the map and you should carry, and know how to use,
a compass.

The shape of Hangershell Rock is determined by the joints in the granite.

There are several tracks leading from the gate onto the Access Land and the route shown on the map uses the one heading roughly north-east. This track joins the tramway at the 'Homestead' **3** marked on the map. At the junction, the wall on the west side of the tramway was built in 1910–11 to protect the Bronze Age walls, some of which would have tumbled into the slight cutting made for the tramway. In winter and early spring, before the bracken grows, the hut circles and their surrounding enclosures west of the tramway are obvious. Near the cast-iron inspection cover on the modern water pipeline there is an enclosure surrounding an inner enclosure with a hut circle at either end. Archaeologists think that from the circular wall of a hut circle a conical roof would have been constructed out of timber with a covering of turves, bracken or heather. If the bracken has grown up you might still be able to find a hut circle a dozen paces west of the northern end of the modern wall.

In the distance to the north-west is Lee Moor china clay works, where kaolin, formed from decomposed feldspar, is won from the altered granite. All the quartz is unaltered and there is much mica and unaltered feldspar so that about 85 per cent of the original rock is waste and is dumped either as sand on the tips or in mica dams. The sand can be used in concrete, for dam walls and as a base for roads, and for replenishing beaches. Some is used locally but the cost of transporting the low-value material means that it usually costs less to dredge sand or quarry it near where it is needed, and so the pits and the tips continue to grow, just outside the National Park's boundary. Over 70 per cent of the china clay ends up in paper, as filler and coating, and indeed china clay is Britain's second most valuable mineral export, second only to oil and gas.

Closer, in the valley, a tiny hamlet can be reached from the path west from Spurrell's Cross to Harford Moor Gate. Harford is thought to come from the Anglo-Saxon 'here', meaning 'army', and 'ford'. The parish church is made of moorstone and is dedicated to the Celtic St Petroc, who founded a monastery at Padstow in Cornwall in the 7th century and is one of that county's patron saints. A walk along the road from Harford, turning right at Torr, will bring you to the camping barn at Watercombe (at grid reference 625613), though if the river is low you might prefer to approach it from the moor. You do this by fording the Erme at the dam below Left Lake and taking the well-used track down to the water-treatment works; as this track continues it passes 330 yards east of the barn.

In places along the route the reasons for the bogs, mires and pools on the tops of hills and plateaus become evident. Just before Hangershell Rock **4** water flows out of the growan, the weathered

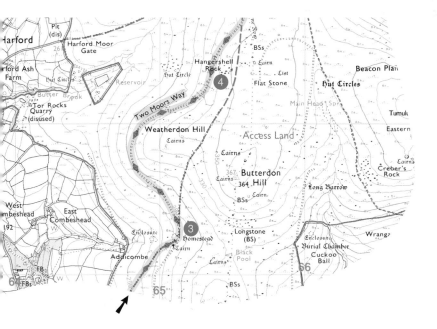

gravelly layer on the granite, and forms a small stream. Above the growan is a thick layer of peat that absorbs the rain, acting like a sponge, but the granite is impermeable so the water can soak in no further. The patch of boggy ground here, though small, has a rich complement of bog flowers among the sphagnum moss with a mass of marsh violets in spring. Hangershell Rock displays the typical cuboid pattern of joints (cracks) related to original contraction as the rock cooled millions of years ago. These planes of weakness are exploited both by the elements to give the rounded pile of blocks typical of tors, and by quarrymen working unweathered granite. The loose blocks of rock below tors and on hillsides are known as clitter.

To the east of Hangershell Rock is a north–south stone row recorded on a 15th-century map of the moor. The row is the boundary between Harford and Ugborough Moors and has had more modern boundary stones added to it. It is nearly 2 kilometres long with over 550 stones located out of an estimated original total of 990. Further to the east, the track shaped like an incomplete running track is just that: a race course **5**, last used in about 1870, when Crossing, who wrote extensively about Dartmoor, recorded that the races were 'attended by a large number of people'. In among all this complexity of remains are cairns and a cist, and to the north a shorter stone row near the medieval Spurrell's Cross **6**, which marks an ancient east–west trackway.

Further on the tramway lies close to the continuation of the long stone row and there are boundary markers **7** with an H on the west face, for Harford, and a U on the east face, for Ugborough. Fifty-five of these were erected in 1803 to resolve a boundary dispute.

The valley of the Erme to the west has a rich collection of settlements as well as much evidence of medieval mining and smelting of tin. The upper slopes of Smalldown Barrow, the hill to the north-west across the valley, show long stripes of loose rock rather than a regular spread. These stripes are thought to be a product of seasonal changes during the Ice Ages when this part of Britain was not covered by ice but experienced tundra conditions as in Siberia and Alaska today. Ravens and buzzards are often seen flying over, and stonechats are common where there is gorse. In the summer, it is common to see wheatear, with their distinctive white rumps, on the open moor.

Leftlake has a china clay works **8** that was abandoned in 1932. Above the tramway are settling tanks and the massive bolts for holding the cylinder of a beam engine in place, and around the bend is the flooded claypit that now has its own characteristic wildlife.

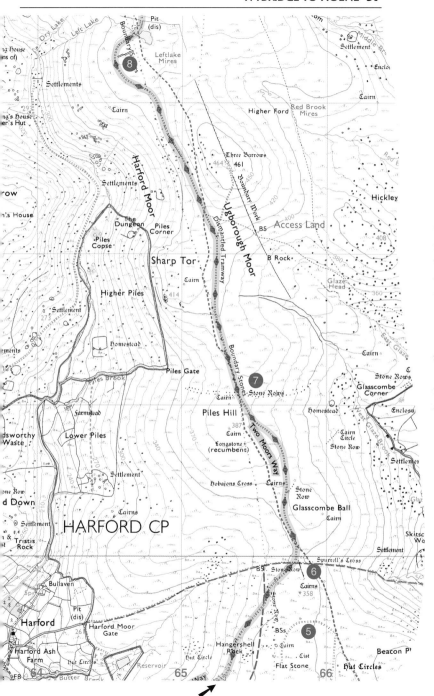

Where the tramway loops round towards the east **9** is a good place to admire the view on a fine day. To the south-west is Plymouth with its naval dockyard and great breakwater, made of 4½ million tons of granite, which was completed in 1841. Another great Victorian engineering feat was Brunel's 1859 railway bridge across the Tamar to Cornwall. Alongside is the 1961 suspension bridge for the road. Further west the headlands of Cornwall jut out, the Gribbin, the Dodman and more. Inland is Kit Hill with the chimney for a tin mine on its summit, and Bodmin Moor beyond. Between north-west and north is the television transmitter tower on North Hessary Tor, a landmark that walkers become rather used to seeing so long as the weather remains fine! Much closer, across the valley, are the scars of peat cutting. The peat could have been used in the smelters ('blowing houses') in the valley bottom, both as a fuel and as a source of carbon to reduce the tin oxide to tin.

Higher up in the valley is the great Erme Pound **10**, which was originally a Bronze Age structure and continued in use into this century for the 'drifts' when cattle and ponies were rounded up for counting and branding. Most Dartmoor ponies are mongrels as a result of 'improvements' and are not nearly so hardy as the original wild stock. True-bred Exmoor ponies are stocky, have a powerful neck and no white, and are very hardy. Nowadays they are used for riding, for carriage driving, and for management of reserves by organizations such as English Nature and the Wildlife Trusts. Many Dartmoor ponies on the other hand end up as pet food.

Further disued workings **11**, but for tin, are further up the tramway and the miners may have located a poor lode. Most of the tin was won from alluvial workings, like the ones in the valley below, where the lighter granite stones were washed away from the denser tinstone. Tinstone, which is pure cassiterite (tin oxide) is about three times denser than granite, so a stream of water is very efficient at separating the two. In the 12th century Dartmoor provided most of the tin used in Europe.

There are more settling pits **12** for china clay before the tramway does a tight loop and the pit and waste tips of Redlake china clay works **13** come into view. The Redlake works was started in 1910 and the tramway you have been following was built from Bittaford, near Ivybridge, to carry men and materials the 7½ miles to the works. The gauge was 3 feet and the wagons were hauled by steam. In all, around 100 men worked at the pit and the settling tanks at Greenhill to the north, but the whole enterprise closed at the same time as the Leftlake pit in 1932.

Just after the ruins of the rectangular stone building with loose red GWR bricks, the Way leaves the tramway on a track to the right

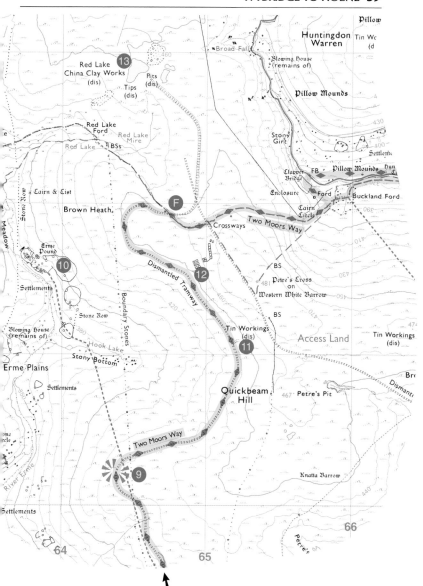

marked by a granite waymark **F** with an incised 'MW' above an arrow. This track is the so-called Abbot's Way, allegedly used by monks travelling between the abbeys of Tavistock, Buckland Monachorum and Buckfast. Historically, the route was known as the Jobber's Path as it was used by yarn jobbers carrying wool yarn on their pack-horses. The connection with the monasteries is that from the 12th century when the Cistercian monks came to Buckfast they had encouraged the woollen industry, and Buckfastleigh retained the industry longer than any other town in Devon as the mechanized factories in Yorkshire were developed in the latter part of the 18th century.

After passing more remains of the china clay industry, at Crossways **G** you cross a sunken tramway, the Zeal Tor Tramway, built to carry peat 3½ miles from Redlake, where the deposit was up to eleven feet thick, south-east down to Shipley Bridge near South Brent. The peat was destructively distilled to form naphtha, which could be burnt or refined further to produce such products as candle wax and naphthalene (mothballs). The horse-drawn tramway had wooden rails bolted to granite sleepers, but the whole venture only lasted from 1847 to 1850 and there are few remains.

The Abbot's Way takes you down beside a tin streaming gulley and as you descend look across the valley at the two prominent round enclosures with three strong humps below them. The humps are the remains of the 'pillow mounds', evidence of a rabbit farming enterprise. Rabbits do not burrow into boggy ground so shallow trenches were cut and covered by stones with soil and turf on top, with drainage channels all around the perimeter. About eighty mounds were made here in all and the rabbit farm, Huntingdon Warren, was in business providing meat and fur from about 1800 to the 1930s. To keep the rabbits in, warrens were built on land enclosed as far as possible by streams, as here, and, where necessary, by walls with vermin traps to catch stoats and weasels. Unfortunately these streams and walls did not keep out the local miners who treated it as a generous take-away: the warrener had to build look-out posts and keep watch at night. Secure inside their warren, apart from occasional predation by any miners and foxes who evaded the warrener, the rabbits had little to do but eat and breed all summer. September to March was altogether different for the rabbits as the warreners harvested their crop with dogs and nets. Some warreners used ferrets and nets, and others nooses or gintraps. But in a hard winter the rabbits did get fed hay.

In the valley you can either ford the River Avon or use the clapper bridge **14**. This method of bridging is very common in granite areas, and has been used at least as recently as 1912 for a new road bridge over the River Fowey on Bodmin Moor. The horizontal slabs on this clapper bridge were worked less than 200 years ago because of the line of half cylindrical holes left by workers using feather and tares to split the rock. Before about 1800 dry wooden wedges had been hammered into holes made by iron jumpers, and then the wedges had been wetted. It is perfectly possible that the bridge is ancient: clapper bridges are recorded from the 13th century. Possibly the original moorstone slabs were washed away in a flood, and better, worked slabs replaced them.

Huntingdon Cross **15** dates from the 16th century and marks the boundary between the Manor of Brent and the Duchy of Cornwall's Forest of Dartmoor. The river flows down into the modern Avon Reservoir, where a rescue dig before the area was flooded found direct evidence of prehistoric tin smelting. Near the cross the Western Walla Brook joins the Avon and you can ford by the cross – if the stream is in spate use the footbridge **H** upstream – and head out across Hickaton Hill, over a dry leat and past the dumps of a tin mine and the well-preserved settlement **16**, to pick up the track from the warren **I** and a choice of routes to Scorriton.

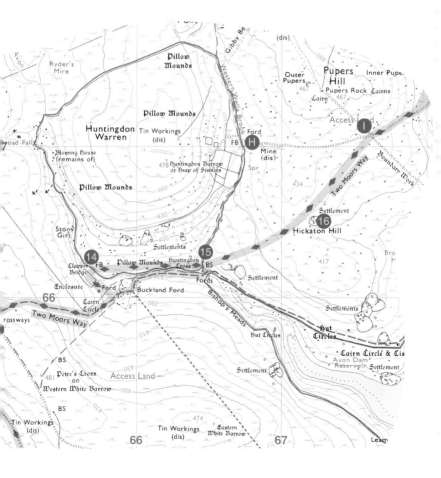

Chalk Ford route

Continue along the track for a short way then walk across the slope between scattered, stumpy hawthorn trees and over wood sorrel down to Chalk Ford **J**, and a wooden bridge and then along a bridlepath the 1¼ miles to Scorriton, skirting the south side of a deer farm on Scorriton Down. The banks of the bridlepath have the usual rich mix of flowers – primrose, violet, stitchwort, bluebells, pennywort, campion, foxglove, etc. – plus a large number of wild strawberries. As you walk down into Scorriton, the pub, The Tradesman's Arms, is worth the diversion of a few paces off to the left, but the Way is to the right and the alternative routes meet at the war memorial **L**.

Lud Gate route

Follow the warren track to leave the unenclosed land at Lud Gate **K** and then at Strole head off to your left through Scae Wood and Lakemoor Wood to Higher Coombe. From Combe ('coombe'), whose name describes its location, you climb up and over the ridge to Scorriton and the war memorial **L**.

From the war memorial the Way is downhill past the phone box, and left at the junction. After crossing the Holy Brook, and passing

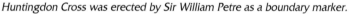

Huntingdon Cross was erected by Sir William Petre as a boundary marker.

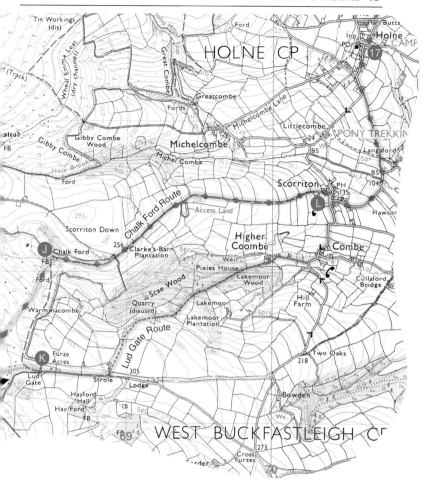

the sewage works alongside, you need to take the green lane - 'unsuitable for motors' – for a steep pull up into Holne, keeping right at the two junctions.

Beyond the church **17** is the Church House Inn, another good pub. This was originally built as the priest's house in 1329, and the rent still supports the church. Charles Kingsley, who wrote *The Water Babies,* was born in the vicarage. The pub has a room named in his honour, with panelling dating from about 1530, which most people may think preferable to the exterior panelling from about 400 years later.

Behind the pub is the post office store, which is also a National Park Information Point. To reach Holne camping barn you need to turn right at the cross-road and walk down the hill.

From above Lud Gate there are views to Lyme Bay.

2 HOLNE TO CHAGFORD

via New Bridge and Frenchbeer   *17¾ miles (28.3 km)*

This section starts using lanes and rights of way and some access land but then you are presented with three alternatives. Which alternative you choose will depend on your interests and the weather. The first two use access land, lanes and rights of way. The western route is convenient for Bellever Youth Hostel and Runnage Camping Barn and Bunkhouse and will take you past archaeological sites, old mines, and good habitats for a range of birds, as well as good landscape. The central route is over the ridge of Hamel Down and is good for archaeology. Finally, the eastern route uses lanes and rights of way and takes you to Widecombe-in-the-Moor and the hamlets on the edge of the moor. This last alternative is the best in poor weather, but if you are particularly interested in buildings you might choose it whatever the weather as you will go through hamlets with superlative examples of granite buildings.

From the church **17** at Holne walk to the dog-leg cross-road and go across and up to Butts Cross and turn left for about 50 yards to reach a stile on your right. The path goes through the fields down to Cleave Wood, part of the National Trust's (NT) Holne Woods property, and on to New Bridge. Below you there are a series of rapids and cascades, including the aptly named Horseshoe Falls **18**, as the Dart tumbles over slate baked by the nearby granite. The mixed woodland here is full of birds. There is a good chance of seeing a dipper flying fast and low above the water, and you might even see one walking under water picking insects off the stones. Dippers are abundant near these fast-flowing, unpolluted waters and the Devon Wildlife Trust (DWT) uses the bird as its emblem. Much of this area is a Site of Special Scientific Interest (SSSI), and while the NT owns Holne Woods on the west bank the DWT has managed the east bank from Dartmeet to New Bridge as a nature reserve since 1967. The main interest is in the sessile oak woodland and the flowerless plants, particularly the lichens.

New Bridge **19** was built in the 15th century and has not been widened: Wallace Arnold, the coach tour firm, has had specially narrow vehicles made to allow them to cross the bridge. From April to October there is a National Park Information Centre housed in the caravan in the car park, and there is often a snack van there too. The public conveniences beside the car park are open all year.

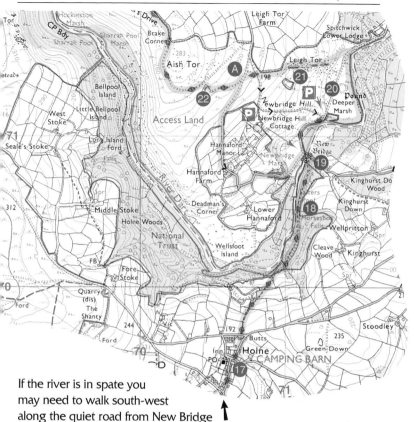

If the river is in spate you may need to walk south-west along the quiet road from New Bridge car park up the hill past Hannaford Manor to a point **A** roughly west of Leigh Tor where you meet the path to the quarry. Normally you can pass under the bridge to walk along the west bank of the river, past the pound **20** hidden in the scrub, until both the grassy bank and the path end as the river swings to the right at the northern end of Deeper Marsh. Cross the road here and take the path heading up the hill. This path soon swings a few degrees south of west, rising to the top of Leigh Tor **21**. This tor is not made of granite but schorl, composed of quartz and black tourmaline. There is so much tourmaline that most of the rock appears black except where it has been cut through by later quartz veins. In a few of the rocks you may see the characteristic dark brown colour of manganese ore and the red of iron ore but the quantities are trivial and there are no records of mines here.

From the tor you need to head west, keeping outside enclosed land and over the road to the track **A** leading to the quarry **22** and Dr

Blackall's Drive running higher up around Aish Tor. The rocks in this quarry are hornfels, a hard splintery rock that owes its character to having been baked at a high temperature due to the proximity of the granite. The closeness of the granite is also shown very graphically by the wall on your right as the overall colour changes from the dark grey of the hornfels to the light grey of granite as you approach Mel Tor. If you are looking for locally distinctive building you could hardly do better! Dr Blackall was a 19th-century owner of Spitchwick Manor and built this scenic drive for his pleasure.

Just after you have turned away from the river at Mel Tor there are some well-preserved Bronze Age hut circles **23** with walls that are still half a metre high. Then follow the wall on your right to the car park and the road at Bel Tor Corner **B**.

At this point the western route splits off from the other two alternative routes. If you use the western route Soussons Farm is 5 miles (8 km) away and Frenchbeer a further 6 miles (9 km). The description of the first part of the central and eastern routes begins on p.56.

WESTERN ROUTE

Walk along the path parallel to the road, and head off across Sherberton Common **C** to circle around the enclosed land, cross the road and then contour back to the road **D** between Yar Tor and Corndon Tor. Heather-topped Corndon Down is access land so you are free to find your own route through to the north end **E**. The route on the map goes close to Ollsbrim **24**, a longhouse set, as is customary, with the animals' half, the shippon, downhill to facilitate drainage and mucking out.

Just off the route, Ollsbrim Cross **25** is a sad sight, armless and holed from when it served as a gatepost.

As you walk up the road you will see low, broad walls, now covered with vegetation. These are reaves, the field system **26** shown on the map. To the left of the road the reaves have become incorporated into present-day field boundaries **27** but this is easier to see before the bracken grows higher than the reaves and almost hides the stone row.

You enter Sherwell **28** past one of the strangest sights on the moor. Hornet's Castle, the house with the gothic windows, is nicknamed Hornet's Chapel and Little Hell. Surprisingly it was a longhouse but the axis, and much else, has been altered. On the left of the road is Sherwell Farm, a longhouse that was rendered in 1947 but which has had the rendering removed. There is a second longhouse in the yard, which is now the slate-roofed barn, and records of a settlement here go back to the 13th century – a common pattern on Dartmoor.

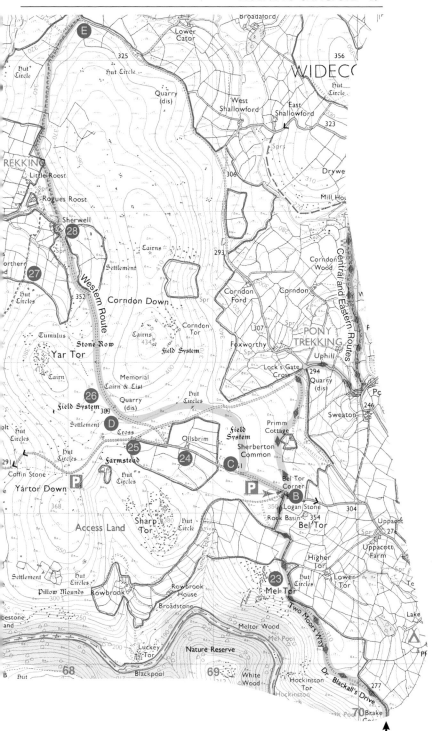

Take the path to the right immediately behind the gothic fantasy. Until ten years ago it was possible to drive a car along this track but up to twenty riders on trekking holidays use this route every day all year with the all-too-obvious result. Do not be surprised if some of the rocks look unfamiliar: someone has dumped a load of pink and grey limestones from Torquay! Torquay must have had really good weather around 350 million years ago when these rocks were formed on the edge of a coral reef. Torquay was south of the equator too.

The track rejoins the tarmac 'county road' **E** at the disused reinforced concrete churn stand, and you need to walk down the road to the gate **F** beyond the windbreak of two parallel rows of beeches. If you want to go to Bellever Youth Hostel continue on this road for 1½ miles (2.3 km), but otherwise take the bridlepath heading generally north to another gate **G**. There are some beeches between the parallel fences **29**, but too few to record on the map. All the straight lines here, including a straightened West Webburn Brook, were the work of Frederick West of Grendon. He was one of the men who tried to make the moor fertile, and went broke.

Runnage Camping Barn is half a mile (1 km) from this gate and you can reach it by continuing to the tarmac road then turning left along the road until the track to Runnage is on your right. A good diversion would be to the stone circle **30**, the closest one to the Way.

From the gate the Way heads easterly on the track. This is one of the church paths that go to Widecombe and along which the 'quick and the dead', in the words of Creed, walked, rode or were carried to Widecombe Church. Many of the church paths join the Lich Way, so called because until 1260 everyone dying in the Forest of Dartmoor had to be buried at Lydford. After that date bodies from this area were taken to the Widecombe Church: Widecombe is an enormous parish, but with very few people. Beside the path there is a boundstone for Cator Manor, incised CB for Cator Bounds **31**, before you join the road at the top of the hill called Ephraim's Pinch **32**. The story goes that a lad called Ephraim was set a test to see if he was man enough to marry his true love. He had to carry a sack of corn all the way to his love's home but at this spot he felt the pinch and was thereafter called a wimp, or its equivalent. Another version has him carrying the sack for a wager. All stories agree that he was a loser.

As you go down the road you will notice that the area around the old plantation of beech, larch and Scots pine has been clear-felled since the map was drawn. Soussons Forest is owned by the Duchy of Cornwall, leased to the Forestry Commission and managed by Forest Enterprise. Most of Soussons is a single-age forest of pine and spruce, but the present policy of Forest Enterprise is for a mixed-age woodland, thereby creating a more attractive forest and increasing biological diversity. Not many trees grow well in Dartmoor's harsh conditions, except in the valleys, so the option of creating interesting woodlands by planting a diversity of trees is not available.

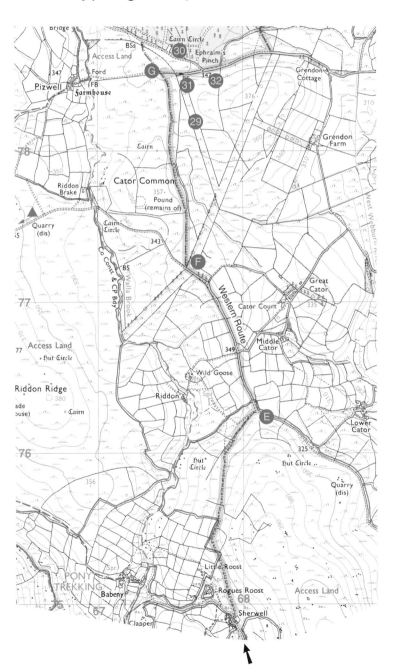

Clapper Bridges are a common feature on Dartmoor.

Down the hill take the gravel road to the left **H** to Soussons Farm **I**, past the sitka spruce, whose leaves are aptly called needles. At least they have a good resinous smell, and these plantations of conifers have brought new birds, such as siskins and redpolls – and in some winters crossbills too – into Devon. In wintertime the wood is a roost for many species. If you want to do some birdwatching, or take a shortcut, at the farm take the path towards Bennett's Cross that skirts the wood and then goes through the wood to Golden Dagger mine, where the routes join **J**. Otherwise, take the bridlepath to Challacombe Farm and follow the loop round the enclosure. To the north-east are the strip lynchets, caused by medieval ploughing, on Challacombe Down. At the bridge cross the valuable stream, and all the marsh and stream-side flowers **33**. In July and August you should see the blue flowers of ivy-leaved bellflower, an uncommon relative of the harebell.

Go over the stile beside the gate and the dog pass and follow the ruts to another gate **K** beside a rowan, a hawthorn and three black-thorn. Challacombe Farm is ahead but you double back on the 'footpath to Bennetts Cross (B3212)', which runs on the uphill side of the fence.

If you walk uphill a little way you will note that the lynchets **34** consist of alternations of steep slopes and shallow slopes. You leave Challacombe farmland at another stile and dogpass at the southern end of the trees. Immediately, the interest changes from medieval farming to mining, for this is probably the most heavily mined area of Dartmoor, even if the known yields have not been great. The first mine you come to is Golden Dagger.

To the left of the track, the round depression with a concrete mound in the middle is a buddle **35** used for concentrating tin ore. The shallow wooden cone like a flat inverted funnel is missing. The crushed ore was fed in with water at the centre of the cone and the water carried the lighter waste, such as quartz and tourmaline, to the edge. To the right is an engine house and other remains dating from earlier this century. You can see where the large bolts held an engine and a flywheel in place. Next you come to Dinah's House, where the miners lived. There is an information board here, installed by Forest Enterprise and Dartmoor National Park Authority.

Within fifty paces further up the path is a concrete wheelpit: this is one reason why the stream was valuable. As well as powering about twenty waterwheels the stream also provided the medium in which the crushed ore was suspended as it was processed. But the processing was not very efficient so appreciable quantities of tin escaped down the stream with the waste.

Near the junction **J** of the bridlepath from Challacombe and the route through the wood is the miners' dry, where the men changed and could dry their clothes.

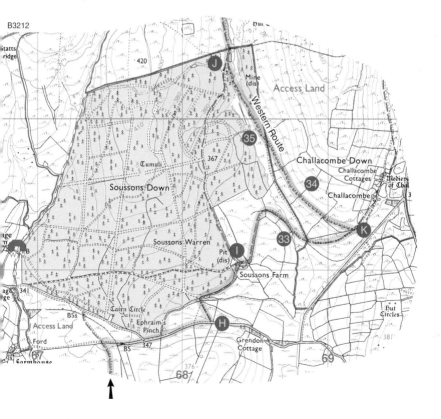

Alongside the path are boggy areas full of sphagnum and a range of bog plants. Further away are vegetated gulleys in the hillside from medieval workings and piles of bare rock **36** beside the shafts of Birch Tor and Vitifer Mine. All the hummocky ground alongside the path will have been turned over for tin as well. Unexploded bombs were brought up from Plymouth in the last war and detonated here, which has further confused an already confused picture.

As a contrast to the mining dereliction, this is one of the best places on Dartmoor to see ring ouzel, the blackbird with a white chest band, as several pairs breed here on the fringe between the deciduous trees and the moorland.

Soussons Circle is the nearest stone circle to the Way, though there are far more impressive ones elsewhere on the moor.

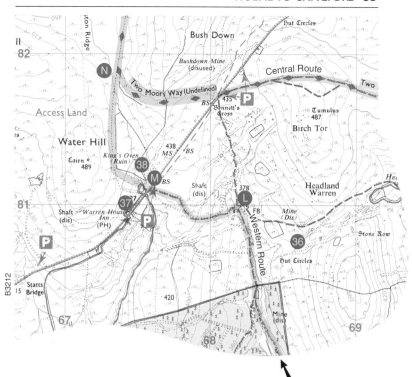

After passing under the electricity cable, two paths cross **L**. The route you have been on continues to Bennett's Cross but now the Way turns left by the buildings and follows the path up the hill, getting nearer to the overhead wires, and joining a cart track as you pass beneath the wires again.

Warren House Inn **37** should now be visible and a path leads off to the left. The true Way passes beneath the electric cables, again, to a small car park on the B3212, where you cross the road **M** with care, and from which guided walks start. The Inn sells dry cider and scrumpy, made locally near Tavistock, so a visit, for research purposes, would be justified.

Head up the eastern flank of Water Hill, where you can pass the King's Oven **38**, then continue down Hurston Ridge, where the central route joins **N**. The King's Oven, or Furnum Regis, is mentioned in the report of the Perambulation of 1240 when a party of knights checked all the boundary markers of the Forest of Dartmoor. Presumably the reference was to a smelter. So much of the stone has been robbed that it is impossible to be sure that the structure identified on the map was really what was being referred to in 1240.

Central and eastern routes

Take care in crossing the Dartmeet to Widecombe-in-the-Moor road and take the track skirting the uphill side of the tree-lined enclosure, then follow the track down to Lock's Gate Cross and the road down towards Ponsworthy and Widecombe.

The top cottage **39** was once a smithy and has wide double doors onto the road. The lower thatched cottages have traditional corrugated iron porches. Ponsworthy has a Post Office and stores, but unless you want to go to the village do not cross the ford or bridge but go through the gate and alongside the West Webburn Brook for Jordan.

In the narrow valley the vegetation is luxuriant: no gnarled hawthorns here. In spring the ground is covered with the flowers of ransoms and then bluebells, and though parts of the wood were once coppiced they are now neglected. At the end of the wood there has been some modern planting with hazel, cherry, oak, elder and guelder-rose.

Cross the stream by the bridge beside the mill house **40** in Jordan. Outside the front door is a collection of granite millstones. Turn right along the road, passing one of the original four manor houses in Widecombe Parish, to the junction then left up the hill. At the cross go over the cross-road. There is a good field maple **41** here that has been allowed to grow naturally, unlike most of the wayside trees in the area, which have been pollarded ferociously, though on the credit side there is a well-laid hedge nearby. The cross, Drywell Cross, has also had a disturbed history. The head was built into the wall on the opposite side of the road, then discarded. The Dartmoor Preservation Association rescued it and mounted it on an octagonal shaft and erected it where it is now, which is probably where it was originally set up. The recess in the head possibly resulted from an earlier use as a slip bar gate.

Go straight on at the next cross-road and as the road bends to the right **O**, the central route heads off over the unenclosed ground of the ridge while the eastern route follows the relatively quiet road down into Widecombe, though in good conditions there is a more pleasant route ahead that will take you down to the village. A full description of the eastern route begins on p.64.

Central route

Head up the ridge, threading through clumps of gorse and probably ponies and belted Galloway cattle as well. On the skyline to the east are Haytor Rocks, the most famous tor on Dartmoor, depicted in countless

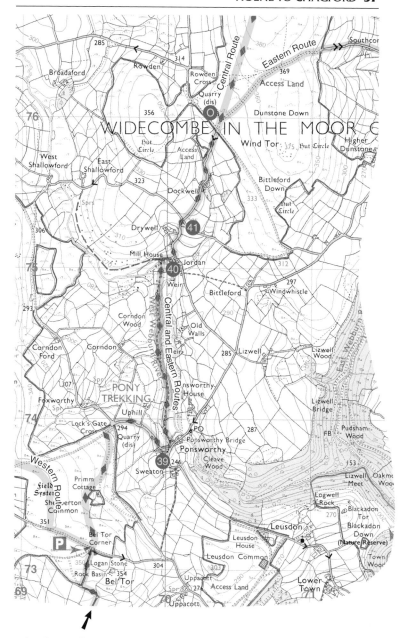

calendars and postcards. All round the tor are quarries that were served by the remarkable granite tramway built by George Templer in 1820 to take the blocks down to the Stover Canal and then on to Teignmouth.

The Two Moors Way is uphill and just before the 409-metre spot height is a natural granite pavement with feldspar crystals up to the size of one's palm. If you wish to visit Widecombe-in-the-Moor, this is the place to head down to the gate **P** from the access land to a lane to the village. On the access land, if the light is right, you may be able to see the lynchets: terrace-like features, which are evidence of medieval ploughing. Soil built up on the uphill side of a boundary and was eroded from the downhill side. You will be able to return on the right of way towards Kingshead **Q**, and to your right, just before the farm, there is a new permissive path that will save you time.

From the summit of Hameldown Beacon **42** the views are extensive on a good day, which is why this point was used as a beacon in Elizabethan times. To the east the light-coloured 'castle' is a folly, Haldon Belvedere, built in 1788 as a memorial to General Lawrence, 'the founder of the Indian Army'. In the distance is Lyme Bay.

In the 1850s the owner of Natsworthy Manor in the parish of Widecombe was the Eleventh Duke of Somerset. Unlike previous owners, and the owners of the other manors, he seems to have been very keen to mark his territory, doing this with specially made round-headed stones or else by having suitable lettering carved on pre-existing markers such as medieval crosses. Hameldown Beacon also had a marker, as 'Hamilton Beacon', and 'DS' for the Duke of Somerset, and the date. Further on, Two Barrows, Single Barrow and Broad Barrow all have the Duke's stones. These barrows and adjacent areas were excavated in the last century and yielded some cremated bones, some charcoal, a bronze dagger and an amber dagger pommel studded with gold pins. The finds and the barrows were similar in style to those around Stonehenge and were dated to about 1500 BC. Sadly, the finds were destroyed in an air raid on Plymouth in 1941.

The Second World War had a more direct effect on Hamel Down as the plateau was considered to be suitable for landing gliders and so when an invasion was feared the flatter areas were studded with wooden poles. A large number still stand. Should they be conserved as examples of recent military activity just as some 'pill-boxes' are being conserved?

Red grouse live on Hamel Down but they have been introduced to both Dartmoor and Exmoor. Their food is the shoots of the young heather, but the moor is not managed for their benefit, unlike some of the moors further to the north in Britain. You may hear their grumbling calls.

Hamel Down Cross **43**, battered and off any known route, also suffered from the Duke's ministrations and now bears 'HC DS 1854'. The

Duke's boundary passes to the north-east through the Grey Weather (misnamed on the map) and Blue Jug stones.

To the west, across the valley on Challacombe Down, are very well defined strip lynchets where medieval farmers ploughed their patch on the hillside. In the valley bottom there are the remains of a medieval village, as well as much evidence of mining and smelting.

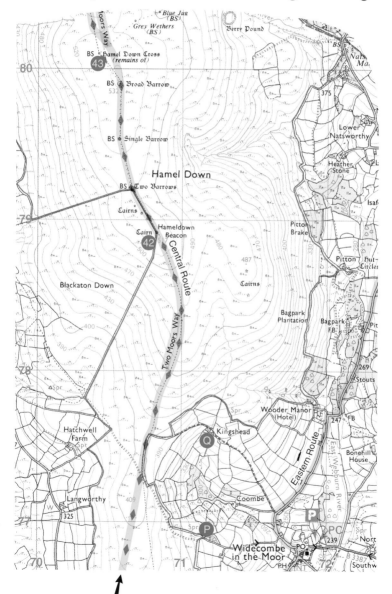

'Warren Bounds': this stone marks the edge of Headland Warren rabbit farm.

From Hameldown Tor the Way goes to Hookney Tor but most people walk down to look at Grimspound **44**, Dartmoor's best-known ancient monument. Until the road was built in 1874 the site remained isolated since it was inhabited around 1300 BC and so probably most of the original stones used are still present, though one hut was modified later, possibly by a tinner. Fifteen of the twenty-four huts were excavated in 1894–5 and the original entrance on the south-east side rebuilt. The other two entrances, on the south-west and north-east sides, have been made by users of the track and are not original. The excavated huts have had their wall stones re-erected: the walls were made of a double ring of large slabs with rubble between. Inside was a raised, paved dais, which was presumably used for sitting and sleeping, and there was a hearth stone and a cooking pit. A central floor slab was possibly a base for a roof support. Through a management agreement with English Heritage, the National Park is responsible for its conservation. One of the problems to be tackled is erosion. The bridlepath through the site does not help conservation either.

Hookney Tor **45**, overlooking Grimspound, is a typical 'cheesewring' tor where the horizontal joints in the granite are much closer together than the vertical joints. The term is derived from a similarity to the 'cheese', the term for the sacks of apples being crushed in a press during cider making.

From Hookney you continue roughly north-west to the road, but below Hookney, and off the route, is Headland Warren Farm **46**. The farmhouse is a longhouse dating from the 14th century though it has been modified, as have all the other longhouses that are still inhabited. From the 1870s it was run as a rabbit farm and in the interwar years three cartloads of rabbits per week were taken to Moretonhampstead for the train to London. Nowadays it is run as a smallholding with accommodation for people, and their horses if required. Evidence for the warrening is abundant and the owners erected at least fifteen boundstones marking the limits of their 1-square-mile warren. One boundstone, with the legend 'Warren Bounds', is by the roadside **47** a few yards off the Way, and after walking across Birch Tor you will find that the medieval Bennett's Cross **48** also has 'WB' cut into it, making the sixteenth. The boundary went from Bennett's to the stream near the pub, the Warren House Inn then followed the wall that is now the northern boundary of the large conifer plantation, Soussons, and across Challacombe Down to the stream, and then follows another wall to the 'Warren Bounds' stone.

The area may already be familiar to you if you are old enough to have seen the film *Run Wild Run Free*, with John Mills, Sylvia Sims and Bernard Miles, which was released in 1969.

Bennett's Cross is also a boundary marker for Buckfast Abbey, for Chagford and North Bovey parishes, and for Vitifer Mine. From the cross you need to head out west
onto Hurston Ridge.

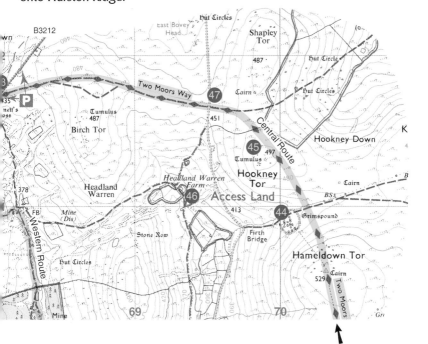

The western and the central alternative routes join here **N** and you should follow the ridge between the North Walla Brook and the Metherall Brook, past a fine double-stone row **49** with a cist at one end. Cists ('kists') are boxes made of stone slabs in which bodies or cremated bones were placed. You will need to keep up high as there are springs feeding the North Walla Brook well above the break of slope, and the springs feeding the two brooks are only a few feet apart to the north-east of the stone row.

To the west is the Forest Enterprise's Fernworthy Forest covering much of the catchment area of South West Water's Fernworthy Reservoir **50**, built to provide water for the tourist resorts of Torbay. One of the problems of Cornwall and most of Devon is that there is virtually no underground supply of water so that winter rainfall has to be stored in reservoirs to supply the vastly increased summer population. Each new application to build a reservoir has created great controversy. At Fernworthy trees were planted on important archaeological sites, including three stone rows and a stone circle, and beneath the waters are a clapper bridge and a packhorse bridge. On the positive side the reservoir does attract some wintering duck, and crossbills and siskins breed in the spruces. The Devon Bird Watching and Preservation Society has provided two hides with a view over the water and marshy fringe, but the water is acidic and peaty with a limited flora and fauna so there is not enough food for many birds. Parts of the forest have been harvested and nightjars use the clearings, though replanting is taking place, but even in its present form this forest is more interesting than Soussons with a bigger range of wildlife.

The evidence of medieval farming and later mining is preserved on Challacombe.

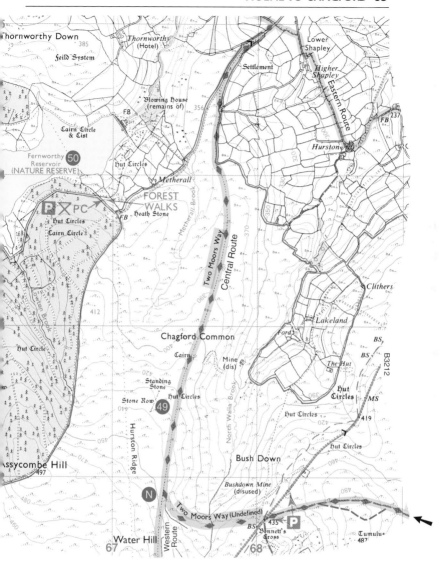

The area around Metherall, shown as small enclosures on the map, has now been planted. The public conveniences are only available from April to October.

The Way joins the road from Fernworthy, and very shortly after you leave moorland Dartmoor by crossing the cattle-grid you will see a stile **R** over the hedge on your right. This is where the eastern route joins.

Widecombe-in-the-Moor is a 'honeypot' full of daytrippers in the summer. The church is well worth a visit.

EASTERN ROUTE

From the bend **O** follow the road down into Widecombe **51**. In 1996 one of Widecombe's cafés had a sign advertising 'seating for 100 inside', which should forewarn you. The church, however, is worth a visit. Whitewashed and uncluttered, with octagonal granite pillars and a floor of granite slabs, colour is provided by a superb collection of roof bosses: green men, a goat, the lion of Judah, St Catherine, a pelican and her nestlings, and many different plants, so take your binoculars! There is even a boss with three hares, and three ears between them, which is said to be a sign of the tinners though this seems unlikely. The church is dedicated to St Pancras, who is alleged by some of the literature in the church to be the patron saint of tinners. St Pancras of Taormina? Cornish tinners certainly held to St Piran, a Celt. The wealth from mining helped to pay for the impressive, pinnacled tower that was struck by lightning during a service in 1638, which resulted in several deaths. Beneath the tower a contemporary record in verse includes the lines:

The wit of man could not cast down so much from of the steeple
Upon the church's roof and not destroy much of the people:
But he who rules both air and fire, and other forces all,
Hath us preserv'd bless be his name, in that most dreadful fall.

Roger Hill, killed in 'that most dreadful fall', has one of the few tombstones in the nave though several hundred people have been buried beneath the flagstones. Later, people were buried in the churchyard, and in the extension to the churchyard is the grave of a William Henry Baskerville. Conan Doyle had been told the legends of the eerie baying of the wisht hounds that foretold a death and came to visit Dartmoor. His touring party had a Harry Baskerville as coachman, and so the legend and young Harry's family name were spun together in this 'most God-forsaken corner of the world', according to Dr Watson, to make *The Hound of the Baskervilles.*

Many people look among the graves for Uncle Tom Cobley's, but the man was buried at Spreyton, north of Dartmoor. According to the song, 'Widecombe Fair', it was the grey mare that he and his seven friends had borrowed and rode that expired, though whether it ever reached Widecombe is not recorded. The song begins:

Tom Pearce, Tom Pearce, lend me your grey mare,
All along, down along, out along lee.
For I want to go to Widecombe Fair.

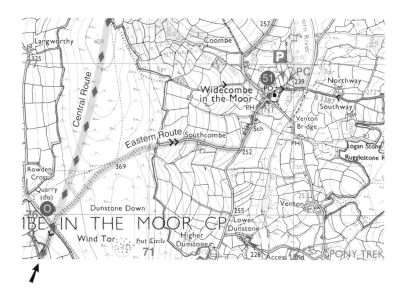

It was published around 1880 and the fair is recorded from 1850. The second Tuesday in September is a day when many avoid Widecombe, though many others flock there for what is essentially now a fun fair.

The 16th-century church house is the parish meeting place and has been used as a school, alms house and poor house, but is now owned by the NT, which uses part of it, the Sexton's House, as a NT shop selling the usual range of tasteful NT products. There is no local produce on sale, though, if pressed, the helpful volunteers will offer you fudge, chutney and honey from other parts of Devon. The volunteers also operate a National Park Information Point, which consists of free leaflets, a wide range of books and local knowledge. Under the arcade is a 15-inch naval shell presented by the National War Savings Committee in 1920 to the people of Widecombe for 'gathering sphagnum moss in the treatment of wounds'. Sphagnum is absorbent and contains a natural antiseptic. Across the road another shop, with, I suspect, quantity rather than quality being the priority, welcomes the hesitant visitor with 'Cum in – tiz viddy yer', though the prohibition on the use of cameras and camcorders has not been expressed in dialect.

East of Widecombe is Haytor, another tourist spot. The granite here was quarried and the stone taken on a granite railway to a canal and then to sea-going ships. The tramway was built in 1820 by George Templer but the quarries closed later that century because they could not compete on price with the granite coming from the Cornish quarries. Before the closure though Haytor had provided granite for many prestigious works,

Orchids are common in damp patches and on verges in Devon.

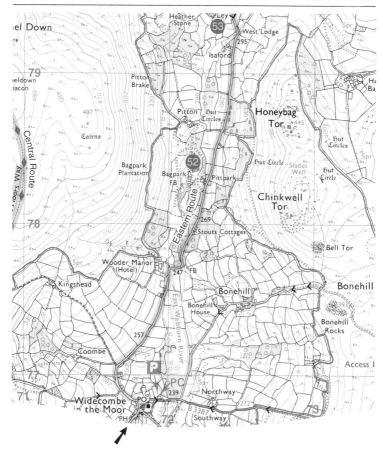

including the New London Bridge opened with great pomp by the young Queen Victoria in 1837. That bridge was bought to span Lake Havasu, a man-made lake in Arizona. In fact, much of London Bridge lies stacked up at Merrivale Quarry, the last working quarry on Dartmoor, as only a thin slice was cut off the granite blocks to clad the new concrete 'London Bridge' in America. Templer's tramway is now the Templer Way, an ideal route for those who like their walking to be downhill all the way!

Leave Widecombe by following the road around the buildings beside the Old Inn and west of the village green. As soon as you leave Widecombe this becomes a quiet lane notable for wild flowers rather than traffic. The valley the lane runs in is wooded, which gives shelter but also hides some of the buildings, such as Widecombe Manor **52**, one of the seven manors in the enormous parish of Widecombe. The first taste of things to come is Ley Farm **53**, a longhouse that you can just see from the road though it is down a private track. Just occasion-ally in longhouses the original internal arrangements in the shippon are preserved: the animals were tethered head first to the wall and their rumps were next to the central drain.

Before passing the gateposts on either side of the road at Natsworthy Gate **S**, you go through the wooden gate on your left onto the moor. Several routes cross here, but, before continuing, if you look to your left, there is a round-headed boundary stone with 'DS 1854' on one side and 'PIT' on the other. This was one of many stones erected to show the boundary of Natsworthy Manor, owned by the Duke of Somerset at that time. The land here has parallel ridges and troughs and though now all grass, these would have been ridge and furrow marks made by medieval ploughmen always turning the soil in the same direction.

Just inside the gate you cross the stream, grandly titled the East Webburn River, and once over the stile you are inside the beech-fringed wood following the yellow paint spots. The Way follows the Mariners Way, which is very well waymarked, so directions have gen-erally been omitted for the rest of the route.

Most of the trees you pass are conifers with a preponderance of Douglas fir and larch, but in these woods many specimen trees have been planted recently so you may come across several different firs, coast redwood, western hemlock and others. Many of the trees are labelled. Beneath the trees the ground cover is mostly moss, wood sorrel and ferns but there is also a good range of fungi. In early autumn you are likely to smell, if not see, the stinkhorn. Once smelt never forgotten, once seen never forgotten: its Latin name is *Phallus impudicus*.

As you come out into the clearing at Heathercombe **54** there is a balsam poplar, which should refresh your nostrils if you have just had a dose of stinkhorn. The final gate into the hamlet was originally a slip-bar (or slot-in) gate. One gatepost into which the bars were slotted is still present. Do not despise this rustic simplicity as the design has sev-eral advantages over conventional one-piece gates: easy to repair and if the lower bars are removed the gate becomes a sheep creep. You will see many examples of slip-bar gates in the next few miles.

Lower Hookner **55** has several interesting farm buildings, includ-ing the barn with a hayloft. There is also the trough for an apple crusher inset into the yard. In the 1970s the hamlet was the base for a pony trekking operation. There was nothing unusual in that except that the visitors were all kitted out in western gear before they rode up onto Hamel Down.

You enter West Coombe **56** past the remains of a waterwheel installed in 1940 to produce electricity and then the path goes round the lower end of the first longhouse. Many books say incorrectly that the right of way goes through the longhouse. The Mariners Way served ale to seamen walking between the coasts of Devon. The house has an elegant doorway in the lower end wall. This is in fact the dung hole and the supposition is that the builder wanted an impressive sight to greet visitors coming up the main track to the hamlet.

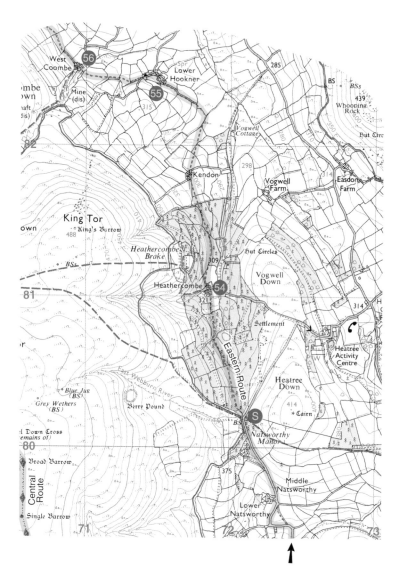

Several longhouses have ashlar blocks, or squared-off granite blocks on the side or corner first seen. The rest of the building is made of granite boulders, 'moorstone'.

You can tell that the houses in West Coombe were once thatched by the steep pitch of the roofs and by the stones built into the chimneys to throw water away from where the thatch abutted the chimney. The Way leaves the hamlet by crossing the concreted yard of the much-altered house with asbestos tiles and plastic gutters that is built along the slope.

As you approach Moor Gate **57** there is the ruin of a medieval chapel above a choked pond full of yellow flag, one of the wild irises. A few feet after you turn right at the first gate there is an ash house half hidden in the garden. This was where the ashes of the winter fires were stored to be spread on the fields in spring. Just inside the main gate of Moor Gate is a gatepost with a circular depression near one end. This gatepost has been recycled from its previous function as one part of a socket gatepost where the gate was hung not from hinges but from a wooden post held top and bottom in sockets cut in horizontal granite slabs built into the adjacent bank.

Moor Gate was originally called Leapra (peasantry), and Leapra Cross **58** was near the chapel, but earlier this century Lord Hambledon removed it to grace his manor house, now the Manor House Hotel. The peasantry revolted and he had to return it almost exactly to the place from where he had taken it. Many of the ancient crosses in Devon and Cornwall have been moved. Victorian vicars often collected them for their churchyards, which was a better fate than being recycled as gateposts or mere wall stone. Nowadays, many crosses are being re-erected, though the original location is no longer known, and sadly quite a few are being stolen, which could be seen as a traditional pursuit. Egyptian obelisks and the Elgin marbles from the Parthenon are just better known.

Take care as you cross the road, dog-legging to the right to the stile off the disused tarmac road.

Lettaford **59** has three longhouses, their associated buildings and a Methodist chapel. Sanders, one of the best surviving longhouses on Dartmoor, is at the lower end of the hamlet and quite distinctive with its porch and huge squared blocks of granite. The house dates from the 16th century and is now owned by the Landmark Trust.

From Lettaford the Mariners Way is often obvious as an ancient route, either as a track or else following a straight hedge line. In places, however, the modern right of way switches from one side of the hedge to the other.

Lower Jurston Farm **60** is another superb building, dating from either the 15th or 16th century, with a fine range of younger barns

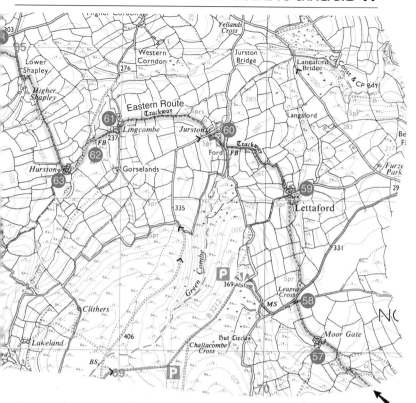

squaring off the yard on the uphill side. The farmhouse has a traditional corrugated iron porch. The Way continues further up the hill between the pebble-dashed house and its barn.

At Lingcombe **61** you turn left along the farm track through the yard then leave the track right behind the house and before the final barn. This path produces a surprise when you walk past a scrapyard **62**. Sam Harris's serves a useful function in being the depository of scrap that might otherwise be spread around, and also it just might have the part needed to keep that old Ferguson tractor going (very green). The path goes over a ford, with a repaired clapper bridge alongside, to Hurston **63**. Here you take the right fork as you approach the hamlet, then turn right around the first house, which has a porch and an Elizabethan window with stone mullions inserted into the wall.

A walk along a green lane and across fields past a very modern bungalow – presumably built to fulfil a pressing agricultural need – brings you to the road **R** to Fernworthy Reservoir where this alternative joins the other two routes.

You can easily miss the sculpture by Peter Randall-Page on the island in the Te

Take the farm drive heading north-west, which leads to Yardworthy and on to Teigncombe and Gidleigh. This route is also the Mariners' Way, supposedly the route taken by seamen between the ports in North Devon and those in South Devon. The parish records of Gidleigh show that alms were provided to seamen in the 18th century but the route, or routes, taken are obscure.

At Yardworthy **64** the first barn on the left has a rounded end, a 'roundhouse', inside which a harnessed animal would have turned a vertical axle and by a system of cogs, belts and pulleys powered machinery such as threshing machines and apple crushers. Leave the yard through the gate behind the house and follow the hedge until you reach a pair of granite gates with slot-in bars. It was probably for a gate such as this that the Drywell Cross was mutilated. Diagonally across the next field is a footbridge across the South Teign river and the Way then passes between two large ash trees and up the hill to follow the boundary of an early 20th-century house, Teignworthy. Further on is Frenchbeer **65**, another farm with a roundhouse but in ruins. The masonry supporting the tap in the second yard you come to is part of a ruined longhouse, and on your left just by the roadside is a rectangular ash house in which the ashes from winter fires were stored to be spread on the fields in spring. Down the road is a thatched house which appears to be another longhouse. Frenchbeer is part of the Duchy of Cornwall estates and has the Duchy's crest, the fifteen gold balls ('bezants') on a shield. These estates have provided the sovereign's eldest son with an income since 1337. Roughly half the National Park is owned by the Duchy, but – contrary to popular belief – less than three per cent of the County of Cornwall.

The Way continues above the thatched farmhouse, through the fields and over boardwalks through woods to Teigncombe. A final gate brings you to a wooden bungalow called Mariners Way and a drive to Teigncombe Cleve. Here the Mariners Way and the Two Moors Way part **T**. The Mariners Way follows the bridlepath uphill signed to Kestor, while the Two Moors Way turns down the lane to continue down the tarmac road to Teigncombe Manor **66**, which is mentioned in the Domesday Book and was remodelled in Elizabethan times. Kestor has attracted archaeologists' interest for 150 years, and excavations in the 1950s unearthed an iron-smelting furnace, forging pit and slag of the first millennium BC in the enclosure known as Round Pound or Roundy Pound. Once past Teigncombe Manor keep left at the junction on the road, which is 'unsuitable for motors', towards Thornhill and on to Leigh Bridge.

At Leigh Bridge the South Teign joins the North Teign, with the restored Leigh Cross **67** perched on a granite outcrop among the

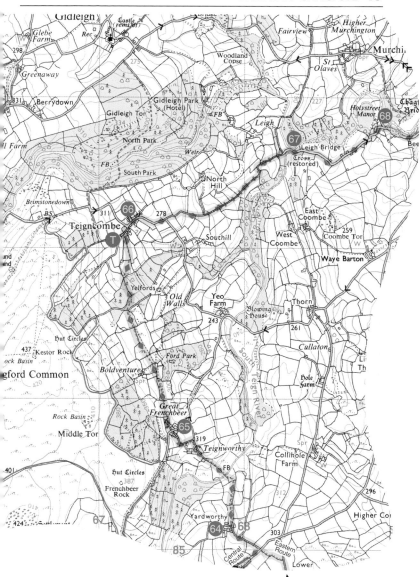

beeches above the road on the right. The Way follows the road down-stream. Medieval Holystreet Manor **68** was 'drastically rebuilt and extended in 1914' according to Pevsner. The front doorway looks gen-uinely old, though the wooden door with its hinges is genuine Edwardian. The 'CAUTION NERVOUS HORSES' sign should be heeded by equine purists. Time for the blinkers?

Devon's clean rivers are the home to dippers, kingfishers and otters. You are more likely to see the dippers and kingfishers than the otters.

Just beyond the kennels is Factory Cross **U**, so called because of the wool factory. Chagford **69** lies straight ahead and is an attractive village but if you wish to keep to the Way you need to turn sharp left and over two bridges before entering the fields. The first bridge is over a leat and the second is the three-arched Chagford Bridge **V** over the Teign. The Taw-Teign Link, one of the link routes between the long-distance footpaths, starts from Chagford Bridge. In this case the other footpath is the Tarka Trail. A leaflet for the link is available from the Environment Department of Devon County Council.

Chagford is a large village but because it serves an extensive hinterland and is visited by tourists it has the facilities of a small town:

places to stay, places to eat, a post office and bank, and shops, including one selling outdoor gear, plus a fine church. If you thirst for knowledge there is an antiquarian bookseller, and, if you just thirst, directly opposite there is a public tap – with a horse trough below. The nearby tea-rooms, not a 'café' in Chagford, is also a National Park Information Point. There is even a small museum in the long-established general store, which displays some of the goods which have not sold after being on display in the main part of the shop for a few years. The store has not been going long enough to display unsold mining equipment, but no doubt in the past Chagford would have provided this as in 1305 it was made one of the original three stannary towns. All tin had to be brought from the blowing houses to be assayed and dues paid to the Duchy of Cornwall. Later Chagford developed a woollen industry, which became mechanized using the power provided by the leats, but the factory closed in 1848. One of the leats has most recently been used for a small hydropower scheme at Factory Cross, which is no longer operating. In fact Chagford was the first community west of London to be lit by electricity.

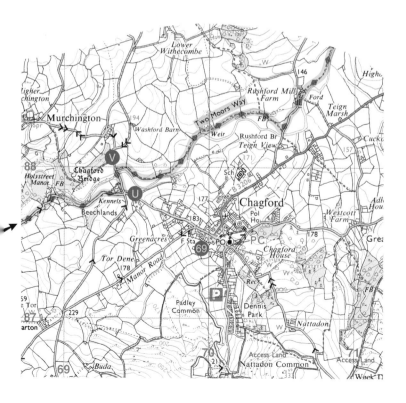

3 CHAGFORD TO MORCHARD BISHOP

via Drewsteignton and Morchard Road   *19 miles (30.3 km)*

The route begins with a walk along the River Teign before you climb up above the gorge. The rest of the walk is through fields, woods and along lanes.

If you go into Chagford you can of course rejoin the Way at Rushford Bridge **A**. The walk from Chagford Bridge to Rushford Bridge is attractive starting from the field by Chagford Bridge where even though a field hedge has been removed the mature trees, four oaks and a beech have been left and have a new role supporting hay-feeders for the sheep. Some sheep fencing holds the hay around the trunk, so shelter and fodder are available together.

Turn left up the road at Rushford Bridge, past an iron seat surrounded by ground elder, recommended by Gerard in the 16th century for gout but cursed by gardeners always. In the hedge you can see the feathery leaves of tansy, a member of the daisy family used by Elizabethans to flavour meat such as mutton; or maybe the strong flavour of the herb was used to disguise the taint of stale meat?

Opposite the open-air swimming pool the granite cottage **70** has a granite pig house on each side; each house has a nicely cut granite arch and window for the pigs to look out of, but they are barred to prevent escapes.

At the mill leave the road by the path to Drewsteignton and Fingle. The mill house has a mill-wheel doorstep, and in the yard there is a circular stone trough of a horse-powered apple crusher.

Further on among tumbled granite boulders on an island in the river is a sculpture **71** by Peter Randall-Page. In autumn this enormous split nut lies among beech masts, acorns and alder cones. In spring the stone contrasts with the greens, yellows and whites of moss, sedge, celandine, buttercup, wood anemone and dog's mercury.

The title of the work is *Granite Song*, which was one of four commissioned by Common Ground to be placed beside public footpaths within a few miles of the sculptor's home.

At Dogmarsh Bridge you enter the NT's Castle Drogo Estate and the parish of Drewsteignton. A short way down river, among springtime bluebells, is a metal footbridge **B**, and the riverside walk continues as the NT's 'Fisherman's Path' towards Fingle Bridge, but the Way leaves

the riverside here and follows the 'Hunter's Path' up through a wooden squeeze-stile towards Castle Drogo. The Hunter's Path becomes a tarmac lane, which you continue to follow as it turns off along a footpath into the NT's Castle Drogo Estate again and climbs towards the castle walls **72**. The NT has cleared much silver birch scrub here and this gives you a better view of the Drewe flag if it is flying. In 1909 or 1910 Julius Drew commissioned Lutyens to design a granite castle for him in what he considered to be the birthplace of his ancestors. Drew had made his money out of importing tea from India cheaply for his growing chain of Home & Colonial Stores. In the process he turned tea into a drink for the masses, and himself into a
very rich man.

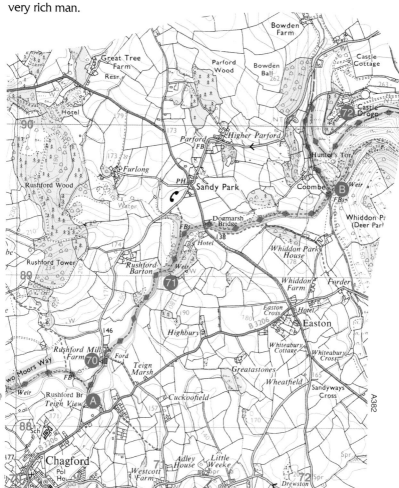

In the circumstance his flag should, maybe, have camellia leaves triumphant rather than a lion passant beneath three fleur de lys on a field of sable. He effectively retired at the age of 33 and indulged a passion to trace his ancestry. A genealogist produced a pedigree which purported to show Dru, one of William the Conqueror's barons, as an ancestor. A descendant of Dru, Drogo de Teigne, founded Drewsteignton in the 12th century. Drogo was merely the Latinized form of Dru. Drew became the more authentic Drewe by deed poll in 1910, and, conveniently, his cousin was rector of Drewsteignton. Even more conveniently a splendid potential site for a castle above the Teign at Drewsteignton was glebe land, owned by the rector. In 1927 Dru's possible descendants moved into their suitably baronial castle, somewhat toned down from Drewe's most grandiose ideas. Julius Drewe died in 1931 and rests in Drewsteignton churchyard, but some of his descendants live on in the castle while members of the NT and those who pay the admission fee walk through the rest. Like most castles Drogo has problems with damp and leaks but the NT has fixed most of these. Unlike most NT properties the contents appear to have been bought almost at random from a very upmarket junk shop: a portrait of Elizabeth I here, some Spanish pieces there, repro French in a bedroom and contemporary Edwardian everywhere. Julius Drew's competitors were the businesses founded by Thomas Lipton and by John James Sainsbury.

After a gentle climb below the walls you suddenly have views from high up over the Teign gorge. There is even a seat **73** carefully positioned for the ideal text-book view of interlocking spurs and a V-shaped valley, though I suspect the reality is rather more complex. Why does the Teign suddenly flow through a gorge?

If you wish to visit Castle Drogo and its garden there are some steps **C** leading to the attractive modern building housing a shop and café.

After Sharp Tor **74**, where vertigo will keep some from the best viewpoints, the Way leaves the valley side **D** but if you wish to explore the Teign further the Hunter's Path goes to Fingle Bridge, overlooked by the defensible Prestonbury Castle **75**, which is maybe 1,500 to 2,000 years older than Drogo.

As you cross the ridge, Drewsteignton lies before you with Exmoor on the horizon. Just as you enter the wood **76**, between the stile and the steps, there used to be a much-used badgers' latrine alongside the path in 1996. Badgers' diet is mostly earthworms but they will eat small mammals and birds. At the bottom of the steep slope a short diversion will take you to *Secret Place* **77**, another of Peter Randall-Page's sculptures.

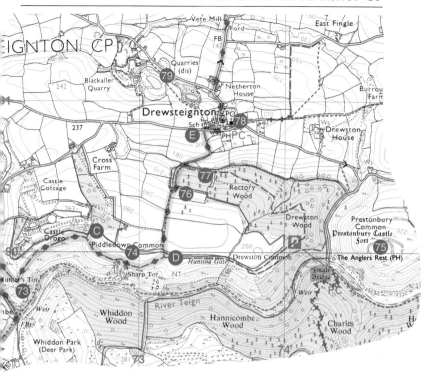

Beside the village allotments the Way joins the road, the junction marked by one of the four Two Moors Way commemorative stones **E**. The precision of the incised lettering is blurring pleasantly towards illegibility as lichen covers the granite.

Turn right here to go through the centre of Drewsteignton **78** with its Post Office shop, church, pub and cob cottages. The church was built in the 15th and 16th centuries. The Drewe Arms is famous among beer-drinking traditionalists for being in a time-warp because of the longevity of the landlady. Sadly, Aunt Mabel has now retired and changes are in the air. Calls for resistance are heard, but realistic rents require realistic prices to be charged.

On the left of the post office the Way takes the road signposted to Crockernwell. At the next junction bear right: the other road leads to the flooded disused quarries **79**. In the early 1850s tunnels were driven to drain these limestone quarries and by chance cut veins of metal ore. In 1854 shares were offered in the Drewsteignton Copper Silver Lead & Tin Mining Company. The prospectus reported very high gold

High above the River Teign the walker has good views back to Chagford.

values from the samples, so it is surprising that a mine never went into production. No doubt the issue went well for the owners – and the analyst was paid well!

At Vete (or Veet) Mill Cross bear left to the valley bottom, then continue over the bridge and immediately take the track to the left marked 'Public Footpath A30 Road', which does not sound too attractive to the walker. Keep every child's dream house on your right and the yard and cottage on your left, and in summer enjoy the scent of the balsam poplar.

The Way is up a damp, close valley, with a smooth black folded tube in black limestone nestling in a niche in a wall **80**, another work by Peter Randall-Page. This one is called *Waterstone*. Badgers find this spot attractive too, scratching for bulbs and tearing rotten wood apart for grubs and beetles; they also use it as a latrine.

Fortunately the traffic on the A30, the main road into Cornwall, rushes by beneath you as you cross the bridge. Then turn sharp right down the lane to the waymarked path before the farm drive. The Way is well waymarked down to the ford and bridge over the Yeo and up to Hill Farm with its old cob house **F**. There you must turn sharp left to pass to the left of a small clump of large oaks. Then, the route is over the fields and across a boardwalk over a boggy patch to Whitethornpass over the fields, a boardwalk that takes you over a boggy patch to Whitethorn, another farm with an old cob house, before you come between two thatched cob cottages onto the road . There you turn right onto the road past the old village school, which functions only as a village hall nowadays.

Hittisleigh Church **81** is a very simple, small, early church made of granite and local stone apart from the simple Norman font, which is made of the so-called Purbeck Marble, a dark limestone full of snail shells. There are no memorials glorifying local scions who put down restless natives. In the church there are memorials to local natives: beneath a granite slab 'lieth the bones of Honor, the wife of Thomas Furse gentleman and Honor the daughter to Honor died October the 4th 1604'. There is a minimal presence of ecclesiastical neo-gothic, possibly because the products of Herbert Read of Exeter, the local church furnisher, were too expensive for the small parish. Fortunate! The only ecclesiastical neo-gothic were 'gifts' from redundant churches, though another gift was the organ cased in simple pitch pine, which is in keeping with the church. The tower is of granite but the walls are of local stones with odd blocks of dark red lava ('trap' locally) and even red sandstone, and the later small windows are made of imported stone.

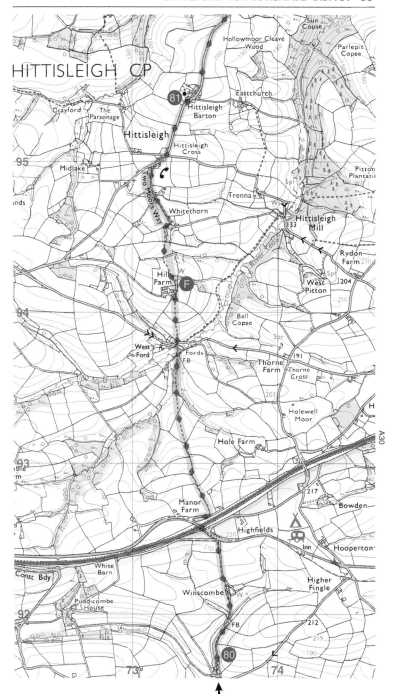

At Howard Cross **G** you have a choice of routes: you can either continue walking along the road on the ridge to the next junction **H** or you can turn left along the lane. If you turn left, at the sharp bend a waymarked path heads off along the side of fields and the edge of a wood with several deer paths to the valley bottom, where you turn right onto the road to climb up to the junction **H**.

At the next junction is a piece of recent industrial archaeology, a milk churn stand **82**, unused since milk began to be collected in tankers in 1978. The Way turns left here but if you were to walk straight on, on the ridge road, in 2 miles (3 km) you would reach Yeoford, which is mostly a modern dormitory village but has a small post office stores, a pub and a railway station on the Tarka Line. The hedges down this lane have a fair amount of spindletree, which has a very hard wood once used for spindles. In autumn the tree bears attractive four-part berries.

Near the end of the lane you walk on a track between small orchards then into the fields and up a steep green lane **83** where water has scoured the soils off the rock revealing the sandstones and mud-stones that run in an east–west belt from Exeter to Crackington Haven on the Cornish coast. At the top of the lane, which is also used by deer, there are fields where the farmer has planted the makings of a hedge along one boundary – not a Devon hedge, which is a great bank of earth covered with plants but a line of hedge plants growing from the usual field level. Of course some Devon hedges are rocky as well.

At the road turn right, past the converted barn **84** made of the same rock that you have just seen in the green lane, with cob on top. Further along the road is Granny's Meadow – surely the topic for a research project in a few hundred years time: who was this granny? If you continue along this road you will reach the village of Colebrooke in 1¼ miles (2 km) but the Way turns off left **I** before the hamlet of Prestons. Go down through the larches of Horwell Wood to the sin-gle-track railway line **J**. This carries ballast trains from the quarries at Meldon. Cross the line with care, and then replace the bars over the stile on the downhill side. Continue through the wood, over the stream and up the green lane, which turns decidedly red. You reach the classic Devon red soil halfway up and pass a badger set. Badgers constantly excavate their set and sometimes rework old tunnels in which dead badgers have been blocked up, so finding badger skulls on the path is a possibility. Their skulls are the only ones with the lower jaw still attached that you are likely to find in Britain. Most peo-ple's acquaintance with badgers is through road casualties: it is esti-mated that 40,000 are killed each year on British roads.

Hedgerows are linear nature reserves.

At the top of the green lane you cross the road to take the tarmac lane to Whelmstone Barton **85**, a cob farmhouse where one of the barns is enjoying a new lease of life under a slate, not a thatched, roof. Pan tiles keep the rain off the top of the cob walls, illustrating the Devon expression about needing to keep cob's head and feet dry.

Walk along the lane towards Ford Farm, but just over the crest the Way turns off left **K**. If you want to visit Coleford or Copplestone carry on past the farm, then turn left at the junction and you will come to a cross-road where Coleford is to the right and the bigger village of Copplestone straight ahead. The latter takes its name from the 10-foot high carved granite pillar, referred to as 'copelan stan' in a charter of 974.

Once through the gate go straight across the field (the hedge has been removed) then across the fields towards the converted coach house below the Tudor Gothic Pashcoe House. Do not go along the drive **L** but keep to the fields as far as Pashcoe Dairy Farm **M**. Old maps and guides may show a right of way along the drive but this is no longer the case.

The route then climbs over the hill to skirt Appledore Farm's buildings **86**. These are of many ages and many materials: cob, brick, concrete block, wood and stone, and show many alterations and adaptations. Where a building no longer has a use and cannot be adapted it is left to decay. The farm milks 200 Friesians in a modern parlour and you may see the cows waiting their shift. The farmhouse is Georgian. Turn left at the end of the drive **N** and if you wish to visit Bow, carry on along this quiet lane. Bow is an early example of ribbon development as in 1259 the local lord of the manor was granted a licence to hold a market and fair on the main Okehampton–Crediton road. Bow has shops and a pub.

The Way is only on the lane for a very short distance and then uses the path across fields to Sweetfield and a recycled granite gatepost used as a bridge. From Sweetfield the Way follows the power lines from the two cottages across a field where the hedge has been removed, and on to Clannaborough Barton. The barns around the farm have all been turned into dwellings, though maybe this influx of new people does not swell the congregation of small St Petroc's Church **87** up on its mound. St Petroc was a Welshman, a Celt who founded a monastery at Padstow in Cornwall, which was moved to Bodmin in 981 after a Viking raid. Very probably he never dressed in a chasuble, stole and mitre as depicted in the window by the lectern.

Cloensbergh is mentioned in 974 and the Barton in the Domesday Book though the present house dates from 1820 and is lived in by the owner of the modern industrial building along the lane. The building is not industrial but agricultural, a swede packer for the excellent swedes grown in these red Devon soils. Swedes from here end up in supermarkets throughout Britain and are even exported to Norway. In the past swedes from the redland of Devon commanded a premium, so less-favoured swedes, say from the neighbouring dunland, were sometimes given a quick bath in a tub of red mud! Rather a versatile vegetable, it turns up in jam and fruit yoghurt, as well as in expected places such as inside pasties.

At the end of the lane take care, for the road here **O** is the A3072, the main Crediton to Okehampton road. Bow is to the left and Copplestone to the right though no one would choose to walk to these

Dog roses come in shades of pink and white, and tiny wasps trigger off an exuberant growth of fuzzy, green galls.

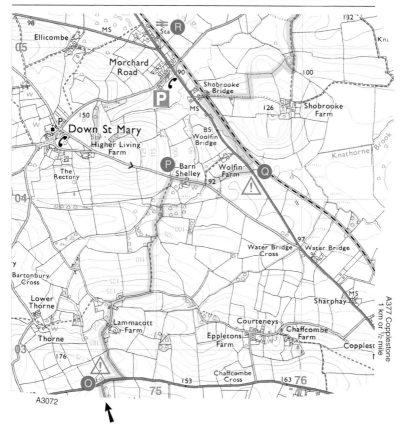

villages along this road. Go right and take the first left up the lane past Lammacott Farm and then continue through fields and a copse to the Down St Mary to Copplestone road **P**. Down St Mary is a very small village but is notable for the Victorian remodelling of the medieval church and also for a cob bus shelter built in 1978 by the local builder.

Down St Mary is to the left, but for the Two Moors Way turn right and then left beside the stream, crossing the field to the A377 **Q**, the main road between Barnstaple and Exeter. There is a recommended crossing point, which is positioned for the longest visibility and with the safety of walkers in mind. The railway is the Tarka Line linking Exeter and Barnstaple with the station that is just a short walk to your left at Morchard Road **R**. To reach the station it is recommended you continue on the Way, on the path by the railway track, to the bridge and then return to the road. The Way crosses the bridge; however, under the 'Rights of Way Act 1932 The British Transport Commission hereby give notice that this way is not dedicated to the public'.

The ponds at Slade have attracted a wide range of residents and visitors; walkers can see much from the path.

The Way follows the metalled farm track to the cattle grid before going through fields to Slade **88** and its new ponds, where wildlife has been allowed to colonize naturally. The single- storey building you see as you leave the yard was once the original farmhouse with a staircase in the rounded corner. The Way does not climb the hill beside the 'new' farmhouse but just about follows the contours before dipping to the stream followed by a gentle climb under a rookery to Weeke.

Dog-leg across the road from Morchard Road towards Oldborough and Morchard Bishop, and beside the grassy island walk between Weeke Barton **89**, an old thatched farmhouse, and the farm buildings. This track takes you through fields and along green lanes to reach Morchard Bishop **90**, which has a couple of shops (including a post office) and a pub. You should be able to buy a leaflet about the village and local walks from one of the shops.

Just as Bow grew up along a road at the expense of older communities so has Morchard Bishop shrunk since the 1820s when a new road linking Exeter and Barnstaple was built in the valley. The new road is now the A377, and villages like Copplestone, once just the site of a cross marking parish boundaries, have grown. The museum in Barnstaple has a poster advertising the new improved coach service. In 1831 you could catch the 'Subscription' from Barnstaple at 'half past eleven o'clock in the forenoon' and after a stop at the New London Inn, Exeter, proceed the same evening and be in London at 4.00 p.m. the next day. The old London Inn in Morchard Bishop is a reminder of when the coach from Barnstaple travelled through the village to Exeter and on to London. There were 2,000 people in the village then, today not even half that figure. The conservation area includes a notable row of 18th-century thatched cottages but probably the best feature of the village is the parish church with its walls and pillars of lava. Nearly all the building is late 15th century: no doubt completion was encouraged by the Bishop of Exeter granting an indulgence to those who contributed to the work. William Easton, a local franklin (a landowner who was not a nobleman) paid for the completion of the south aisle where he and his wife now rest below their effigies. Indulged or not, the Eastons were obviously doing well at this time as they also built themselves a new house at Easton Barton, which they owned for at least a century more and which survives almost unaltered to this day.

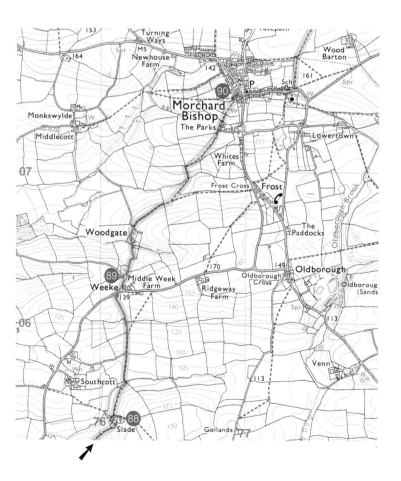

4 MORCHARD BISHOP TO KNOWSTONE

via Witheridge   14½ miles (23 km)

This section is through a land of scattered farms with no villages apart from Witheridge. In addition to the two pubs in Witheridge itself there are another two fairly close to the route, and close to each other, as well as pubs at each end. Several of the farms do bed and breakfast but it would be a good idea to check that an evening meal is available: from most of them it's a long walk to a pub!

The Two Moors Way leaves Morchard Bishop along Church Street and after the church you go past another Two Moors Way granite marker **A**, through the school car park and across two fields; then turn right over a stile (galvanized in 1996) **B**. Do not follow the path diagonally into the nearby Morchard Wood of conifers fringed by oak and beech, but follow the metal fence line on your right until the Way strikes off left diagonally along a slight ridge, the vestige of a hedge now removed, to the stile and waymark by a large maple **C** and a patch of snowberry. Morchard is one of the few Celtic names on the Way and is

The first walkers across the newly ploughed land trod a wandering route!

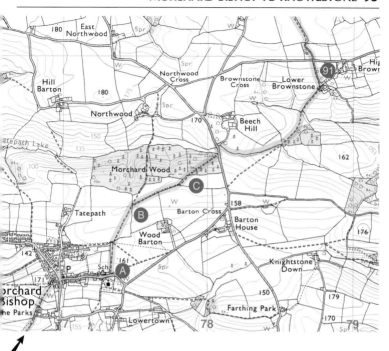

derived from 'mor cet', great wood. Most of Devon is thought to have been moorland or woodland in the 7th century before the Saxon occupation and this 'great wood' must have been a major feature, possibly stretching the seven miles or so to Cruwys Morchard and beyond. The addition of Bishop to the village's name arose because the manor became the property of the Bishop of Exeter in 1207.

The Way goes through a plantation of spruce with wild raspberry below, followed by beech and a carpet of wood anemones in the lower part. In another part of the wood Douglas fir is harvested by Fountain Forestry for three-by-three and four-by-three fence posts. While versatile, spruce is not as valuable as timber, although spruce is often preferred for paper-making because of its lack of colour and long fibres.

Dog-leg across the road and along the fields, keeping above the valley bottom, swing left towards Lower Brownstone, then cross the stile and the stream, then up the hedge with the badgers' set to skirt the farmyard of Lower Brownstone Farm. To the right of the farm lane is an old apple orchard **91**, with many trees recumbent, pushed over by cows years ago, but still bearing fruit. Cider was made from the fruit within living memory, but nowadays most of the fruit is eaten by the sheep who rub the trees to get the apples to fall.

Cross directly over the road, passing a patch of white comfrey, and walk – or run – up the bright grey limestone drive of the dog kennels to the accompaniment of a cacophony of howls and barks, then pass over the stile and into the fields to cross the stony stream by a bridge. The patch each side of the bridge is swampy after rain and short on stones to step on, but at least the rich yellow of the kingcups may lift your spirits if the waterproofing of your boots is found wanting.

The steep slope of the next field, with its lone apple tree, does not appear to have 'enjoyed' 'weed and feed' recently, and so there is a wide range of wild flowers. In a very few yards, as you reach the flatter part, the diversity drops: a sign of improvement. As you cross the next stream you step into the parish of Woolfardisworthy, a good Saxon name, which is pronounced 'Woolsery'. Up the hill is Wood **92**, where you pass a linhay, an open-sided barn, made of breeze blocks, and then the cob wall of an old barn, built on stones, 'to keep its feet dry'. The layers in the wall are obvious, formed as the cob was built up, then left to dry before another layer of red, stony soil mixed with chopped straw was added.

Further on an isolated corrugated iron barn **93** in 1996 was full of abandoned machinery: an old Massey Ferguson combine harvester (780 Special) with guarded chain and cogs, and a sign advising 'Safety First'; and an even older threshing machine, with unguarded belts and a plate attesting to a main shaft speed of 1050 revs per minute. Blood splashes from accidents would have shown up prominently on the delicate cream paint, though less obviously on the red part of the colour scheme. Before combines, corn was cut, stacked in stooks to dry and then collected in and threshed. Agricultural contractors used to tow machines like this from farm to farm at harvest time. Today combines do the job in one, and grain is put in a grain dryer.

Cross the lane, some more fields and another stream to Cobscombe Farm and the lane **D** at the end of the farm drive. The Way turns right here but there is a good pub at Thelbridge Cross about one and a half miles to the left, past Hele Barton.

This area is known as Black Dog, though whether this refers to a hound or a Churchillian depression is not recorded. The Black Dog Waste Water Treatment Works, using a reed bed and a solar panel to power the instrumentation and telemetry, obviously is more recent than the wartime leader. The pub – yes, called The Black Dog – at the cross-road predates him. The local television station found it amusing to fill gaps by showing clips of the sign on the pub door which informs prospective clients that they are welcome but dogs are not, unless the latter are guide dogs. In 1996 the pub was not open at lunch time except at weekends. There is no shop: it closed. There is a telephone box at the cross-road, but beware of locals cutting the corner at the cross-road if you use it.

The Two Moors Way does not explore Black Dog, let alone the hamlet nearby called Tree **94**, but leaves the road at the end of the garden of 'Oaklands'.

Things look up as you approach Pyne Farm **95**, an attractive house originally built at the time of the Armada and gentrified later with a cob-walled garden in front. All the buildings necessary for carrying on agriculture are to the side or at the back.

Cross the valley **E,** aiming aim for Wonham, the farm facing you, rather than towards Sentrys, which consists of the red brick house and the bungalow. After Wonham, follow the field boundaries above the valley bottom until a waymark at the corner of a field fenced with concrete and wire heads you down to a bridge **F** and into the wood. The first part is a disused coppice mostly of oak, whose bark would have been used for tanning, and finally walk beside
a hazel coppice

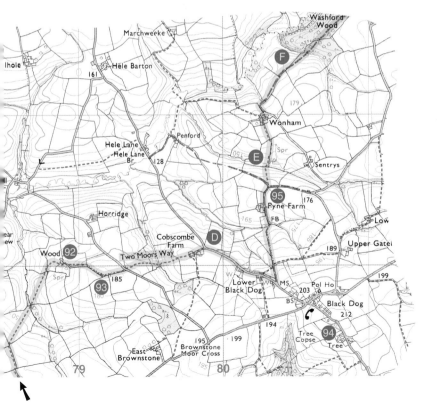

to the lane where you turn left to Washford Pyne **96**. The small church was rebuilt in the 1880s after a fire effectively gave a local Victorian church architect a free hand.

The Way goes between the church and the Georgian rectory over the fields and Henceford Brook to Stourton Barton **97**, the home of 140,000 broiler chickens in 1996. Broiler chickens are slaughtered at 42–3 days on average, and the UK market is 700 million birds a year, rising by 2–3 per cent per year. Walkers will see the occasional chicken scratching around one or two farmyards. Further on, the ponds either side of the tarmac farm drive are home to a small flock of Canada geese. In the wild their life span is around ten years. If the geese are not there they have probably commuted to their second home, a pond near Witheridge – an agreeable lifestyle. By the road is another clutch of broiler houses, one bearing the warning 'Disease Precautions KEEP OUT No Unauthorized Personnel to Enter this Area'. The automated controls cut in and out to optimize the chickens' conditions.

Pyne Farm is a good example of a cross-passage house dating from the late 16th century.

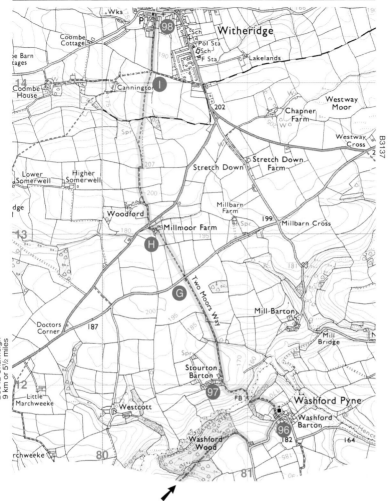

Cross the Chawleigh-Tiverton road **G**, where Thelbridge Cross and its pub is again a little over one mile to the left though there are pubs not far ahead in Witheridge. To the right is one of the many places in Britain called Nomansland, places between parishes where those who killed themselves were buried. Nowadays this Nomansland has a pub called the Mount Pleasant Inn, a suitable name.

Cross two fields for Millmoor Farm and go between the farm and the bungalow **H** to Woodford's farm lane and the fields beyond. Exmoor should be bold on the skyline to the north and Dartmoor to the south as you pass the junction with the Little Dart Ridge and Valley Trail **I** and then drop down to Witheridge **98**. The first contact is the bungalows in

Wiriga Way. Cross the road at the end of Wiriga Way and take the path between the bungalows, go past the long gardens of the 1840s terrace of rendered stone houses until, suddenly, you enter the village square beside the post office. 'Sleeping, cooking, camping, personal ablutions and disturbances likely to cause a breach of the peace PROHIBITED' is the welcoming sign in the village square, which has also been spoilt by a public convenience block made of 'reformate', a reconstituted stone.

Witheridge is like Morchard Bishop: bypassed. In Witheridge's case the disaster is very recent, caused by the North Devon Link Road, the A361, which joins the M5 near Tiverton, though the buses still come this way, almost empty. Witheridge square dates from Saxon times and was the site of a weekly market and a three-day fair dating back to 1248. In the 1890s the village had two fairs and three great cattle markets annually, and until recently there were four pubs on the square. Nowadays Witheridge is so quiet there is likely to be no one at all in the square, let alone people indulging in prohibited activities. But it is worth exploring the village. On the east side of the square there are some limewashed cob cottages, still with their thatch and separated by narrow alleys, and there are signs of Victorian prosperity. At the present time there are a couple of general stores, including the post office and the baker, but the butcher and the bank have closed since the new road was built. On the edge of the village are new industrial units to provide new jobs, but Witheridge's greatest success must be the bridal wear factory, Romantica, which exports 80 per cent of its production.

Cross the square, go right round the Angel Hotel and continue past the Mitre Inn, which was built as a coaching inn in the 1830s but the old entrance for coaches into the yard now has a large and rather severe-looking gate. As you turn left on the Rackenford Road the village baker (in existence on the site for over 700 years) and a furniture restorer cum second-hand book shop are behind you. Past the Parish Hall and just before the road divides, the Way is through a kissing gate and through fenced-off grass and alongside the parish playground. This short strip of grass, best described as the parish dog loo, ends at another stile that leads the walker into fields where even the most casual observer can see most dog walkers do not venture. Another stile brings you to the green lane and fields, and then to Yeo Copse **99**, owned by the Woodland Trust and carpeted with bluebells in May. This was formerly oak coppice but the new management will produce a wood of big oaks good for about 500 years.

Walk down to the river just above a ruined weir, which controlled the leat for Witheridge Mill. You can ford the tributary brook by the stile or follow the alder-lined meanders to a plank bridge, and then walk upstream.

In 1996 recycled galvanized pail handles were the local fashion for gate catches here! Above the stream a bulldozed pile of stumps and a line of a few living oaks, one with a severed ivy thicker than a man's calf, bears silent witness to a grubbed-out hedge. Ivy is nowadays seen as providing good cover and a good food source for insects and birds, and as healthy trees can outgrow ivy so the passion for severing ivy is past. Across the river the ponds are rich in wildlife, and through the trees you may catch a glimpse of a heron or duck. The river is used by otter and you may be able to see the spraints (droppings) on prominent rocks, and footprints in the mud.

The conifer plantations provide good daytime cover for deer, which have made very clear paths as they come out to feed on the marshy, rushy fields **100**, and you may be quiet enough and fortunate enough to see fallow deer grazing by day. Turn left onto the road, by the two semi-detached houses in rich honey-brown stone with slate roofs. The end wall facing west is also slate hung to protect it
from the worst weather.

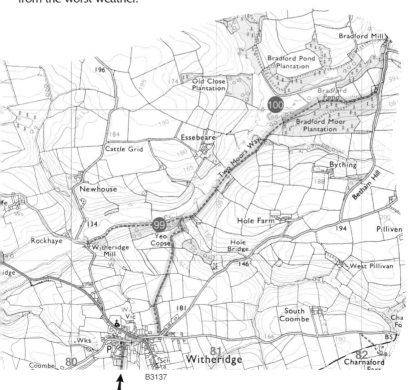

Bradford Mill **101** was working as a mill in the 17th century, along with Witheridge Mill and Drayford Mill, but only Bradford Mill continued working into the present century. Up the hill the cob gatehouse to Bradford Tracy House has a circular outside toilet **102** with a slate roof beside the formal gates. The loo is a listed building.

At the junction, Bradford Cross, take the road to Creacombe and Rose Ash. On the left is the 5-acre cider-apple orchard **103** belonging to Bradford Barton.

Crowdhole Cross is the next junction: continue on the main road (this term is relative!) to Creacombe and Rackenford, and at Parsonage Cross bear right to Rackenford (3 miles). These lanes have wide verges and what appear to be at least three grown over ponds so, probably, this was a drove road for taking cattle to Witheridge market. At Creacombe Moor Cross continue towards Rackenford.

One of the farmers has planted a few native trees (beech, oak, ash, lime and cherry) behind a new bank in the corner of a field. Modern machinery could not work into this corner so a waste of land has been turned into a gain for wildlife. The Farming and Wildlife Advisory Group produces a range of leaflets, and much personal advice, should farmers want it. By implementing such schemes the image of farmers improves with the public too. At the next road junction there is an obvious toll-

Witheridge is worth taking time to explore.

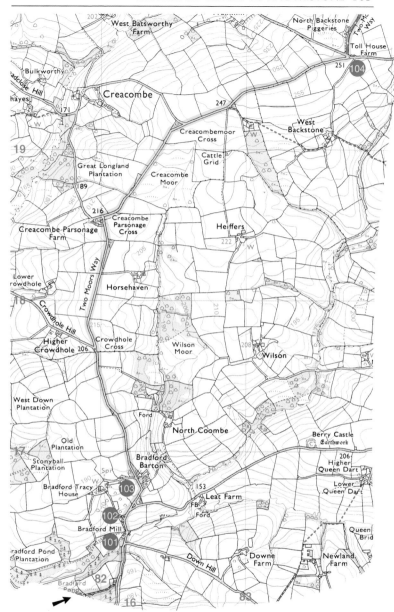

house **104**. The road is quiet now, with traffic from the little village of
Rackenford occasionally disturbing the peace, yet in the late 18th century this was the main road between Tiverton and Barnstaple.

Cross the road and go down the green lane. Fortunately for walkers and residents, the North Backstone Piggeries shown on the map have now become the Backstone Moor Mill of the Clean Feed Company. The beech trees and a few oak support a large population of grey squirrels – 'tree rats' to some – which are unperturbed by humans, and before the trees are in full leaf it is easy to spot the squirrels' dreys. Black 'bootlaces' under the bark of dead trees indicate the work of honey fungus, which possibly performs the same role in finishing off old, sick trees, as pneumonia, 'old man's friend', does in humans. The fungus caps make a rich and delicious soup. The dead trees are drilled by woodpeckers searching for beetles and grubs. The green lane opens out onto Knowstone Outer Moor, damp heather and gorse, willow and birch. Ahead, vehicles on the North Devon Link Road, channelling traffic from the M5, mask the sounds of the countryside for most of the day and much of the year. Turn left on the road across Knowstone Moor, slowly getting closer to the link road, go past a sign to Great Comfort Farm and continue over the Sturcombe river to cross the roadside fence **J** by a wooden stile and then cross the road. Take care! Many walkers choose not to risk their lives on the crossing. Opposite the last metal drain at the edge of the road take a path to the right across the moor. This runs in a serpentine fashion through the gorse parallel to the road (you may indeed see some serpents, or at least lizards). Pass beside the Sturcombe River under the concrete bridge, with the traffic drumming on the expansion strips above. The route back to the official Two Moors Way is boggy but has willow herb and bog violet to counteract the fumes and noise of the traffic. Rejoin the lane, which was cut by the link road, and carry on to the cross-road.

The moor **105** is both a SSSI and a DWT reserve, managed by grazing and burning. 'A piece of Devon for Ever' as the DWT board proclaims. Until the enclosures of the 18th century much of the area between Dartmoor and Exmoor would have been similar, a mixture of wet acid grassland, heath, bog and scrub. Hardy native animals, the sort the Rare Breeds Survival Trust conserves, would have grazed this. One of the hardy animals is the Ruby Red, the local North Devon cattle, which graze another of the Wildlife Trust's reserves at Meshaw a few miles away. These nearly became extinct though a few bulls continued to be used to produce good beef calves from Friesian cows. Nowadays the breed is anything but endangered although there are probably more Ruby Red genes in Brazil and New Zealand than in Devon, and ampoules of semen continue to be exported to increase the stock.

One mile ahead is Knowstone, but as the road steepens to drop into the village the Way takes off on the right inside the hedge to the churchyard, behind the old school with its bell, to the pub, the Masons Arms,

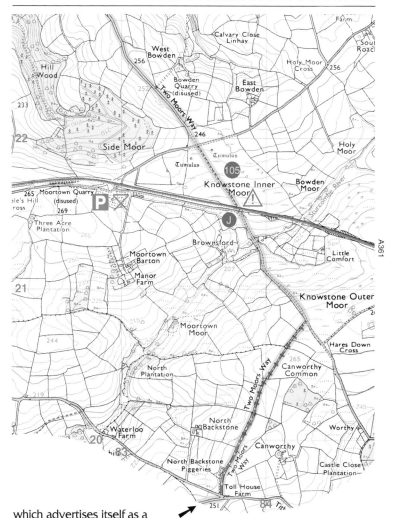

which advertises itself as a
'C13 Residential Inn'. The village
also has what must be one of the prettiest post offices in Britain. This
rather makes up for the church. In the last century Parson Froude distin-
guished himself by his lack of interest in his parishioners, unless they
hunted, fished, shot or drank. As a boy R.D. Blackmore, later the author
of *Lorna Doone,* knew the parson and tells the story of a chase when
the fox went to earth. This act jogged the parson's memory and he said
that he had 'a corpse to bury at three o'clock, and I shall already be an
hour late!' Just outside the village is Great Wadham, an old farm con-
nected with the founder of Wadham College, Oxford.

5 KNOWSTONE TO WITHYPOOL

via Yeo Mill and Hawkridge 12½ *miles (20 km)*

This is a gentle walk through fields and along lanes with two alternative routes for the last part into Withypool. The better route is via Tarr Steps and along the east bank of the Barle, but if the river is very high Tarr Steps may be impassable, so the alternative is over Withypool Hill, then crossing the Barle at the bridge in Withypool.

Leave the village **106** with the Masons Arms on your left and go to the road junction, Greenhill Cross, where the Way follows the road left to Owlaborough and past Highfield Farm. Bear left along the lane, and where the lane turns sharp right you enter a narrow field that is mostly a scrub of willow, hazel and birch with a surprising variety of cultivated daffodils beside the track. Up the hill as the ground gets dryer, the scrub changes to gorse and bracken then back to willow. At the top a scatter of abandoned machinery includes a wooden- and metal-framed roller and a patent Martin Cultivator; the design winner of a first prize at the 1900 Royal Agricultural Society of England. Only the seat and the horse are missing. A relic from the fibreglass era is also in this informal museum **107** of agricultural heritage.

From the barn the Way cuts across the fields of Owlaborough Moor to the plantations, now mostly a regrowth of small birch, and the road **A**. A few hundred yards to the right is the Jubilee Inn, but the Way only makes a short dog-leg before using a permissive path over Easter New Moor for the next road at Highland Head Cross. Take the road toward Yeo Mill and West Anstey. The road cuts the old Taunton–Barnstaple railway line **108**, which was originally built to Brunel's broad gauge (7ft ¼in) but which in 1880 was converted to a standard gauge (4ft 8½in) over one weekend by an army of navvies. The line was closed in the 1966 Beeching cuts, the tracks lifted and the land sold. In Yeo Mill **109** the Partridge Arms had a bad chimney fire in 1880, and the lintel is now made of two broad-gauge sleepers, admittedly cut down a little by a later door opening. The Partridge Arms is named after the Partridges who were major landowners in the area and nowadays it is run as a farm with over a thousand Exmoor Horn sheep, but the farm still uses its residential licence.

The village of Yeo Mill also has public conveniences, a telephone and post office stores. At Yeo Mill Cross turn right towards Wychwood and Dunsley. A quarry **110** probably provided some of the red sandstone

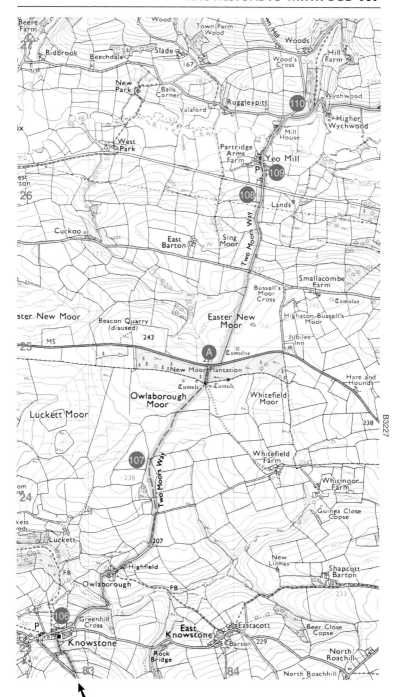

so prominent in the roadside barn at Partridge Arms Farm. On the other side of the road a horse-drawn hay turner, by Denning of Chard in Somerset, has been put out to grass under a sycamore, but the walker may be more aware of the roadside ransoms, a member of the garlic family. In spring the young leaves are good in omelettes; later the taste, and smell, are rank.

Behind Higher Wychwood is a small patch of conifers with a Douglas fir dropping its cones with three-tongued bracts on the road.

The Way leaves the road up a bridleway that climbs steeply to end at a stile over the crest of the hill and some carefully laid hedges but with rot-proof binder twine replacing the traditional wooden pegs. The new Elizabethan Plantation 111 was planted in Tree Week 1992 to celebrate the 40th Anniversary of the Queen's accession to the throne. A very small sign also points out that the planting was organized by the Farming & Wildlife Advisory Group and sponsored by the Tree Scheme run by the local electricity supplier, the SWEB. Children from the primary school carefully planted hazel, field maple, dogwood, rowan, oak, ash, crab apple, lime, copper beech, beech, and birch in this fenced-off corner, but a year or two later the sheep got in and did some pruning. Pruned or not, oaks can live 500 years and it is a moot point as to what form of political system might be current in the British Isles when these are mature. There were petty kingdoms throughout these islands when many of the churchyard yews were young. And in the garden of West Anstey's Old Vicarage 112 the flourishing Wellingtonia, thought to have been planted in the 1870s, would have been young when the British Empire was colouring more of the map red. But long before the cherry was planted by the road to the church, villagers would have dipped a bucket into the shallow well for water. The cast-iron pump, attached to the lead riser, also predates the cherry.

Here a diversion off the Way to the church 113 is worthwhile. The churchyard has a range of Victorian memorial poetry and the church, despite a far-reaching renovation in 1879, has some features not seen so far: a squat dog-tooth and cable Norman font, some fragments of medieval glass and some Tudor bench-ends. The pink colour wash is unusual, and the precise passion flowers on the capitals of the new light-coloured stone from Ham Hill contrast with the generalized leaves of the dark medieval capitals. Note too that the cult of the Mission Statement has reached St Petroc's, West Anstey. Some walkers might be trying to escape this particular cult for a few days.

As you climb up Badlake Lane the banks are full of wild strawberries, and also the whortleberry, a moorland plant, re-appears. Badlake Moor Cross marks where the Way enters its second moor, Exmoor. The change

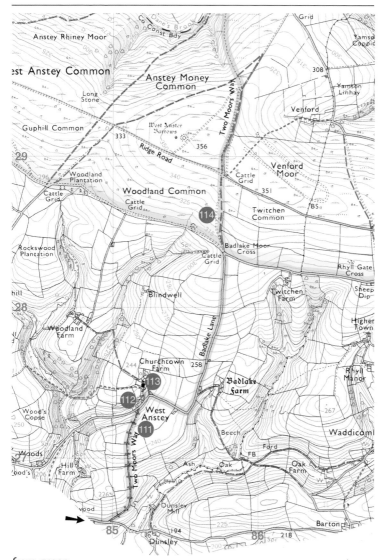

from green
grassy field with
neatly laid beech hedges to open moorland **114** with gorse and
scrubby trees is dramatic. There is no geological change here: it is
purely man-made. In a few yards the moorland becomes more interesting with different types of heathland, and birds such as whinchat,
stonechat and wheatear. This area is one of the five blocks of heathland
that make up the South Exmoor SSSI.

Once over the cattle grid waymarks are less frequent. The way to the next village, Hawkridge, shown by an old finger post, 'Hawkridge 3', is either to follow the track with the hedge nearby to the right or else the more frequently used strong track skirting the road. The tracks rejoin further on at the next road. The Way follows the bridleway indicated by a fingerpost, 'Hawkridge 2¾'. As the bank turns more easterly after the end of the bank-top beech trees, the Way veers left off the bridleway, down to Slade Bridge. Anstey Money Common preserves a relic of the name of the local Norman barons – Le Moigne. Any ponies here may end up at Bampton Fair on the third Saturday in October, a day for real trading unlike the present day Widecombe Fair.

The bridge **115** marks the boundary between West Anstey and Hawkridge, and also between Devon and Somerset. At an S-bend in steep Slade Lane the Way starts to recognize contours by taking the bridleway to Hawkridge, first across a field to West Hollowcombe, then the lane to the copper beech that shades the seat and a pump at the junction. There is a telephone here and also a house called Moor View **116**, where in 1840 the Lock family began making gates and carts. While his sons still make the gates, Tom Lock now makes horn-topped walking sticks of blackthorn or ash so if you want a traditional countryman's accessory you could buy one from the maker here. The Way turns left up the hill at the junction but a short walk to the right takes you to Hawkridge Church with its Norman doorway with simple zigzag carving, and – to bring the church right up to date – a Mission Statement. This one was for the Diocese of Bath and Wells. If you were to carry on past the church and down the track called Row Lane you would be on the Exe Valley Way, 45 miles (72 km) through Dulverton, Bampton, Tiverton, and Exeter down to the South West Coast Path.

The Two Moors Way leaves the road **B** by the letterbox and behind the post office. Cross the first field to the hedge-top beech tree, then two further fields and walk first along the top of the wood, then along the old, faint field boundary following the contour. The Way then leaves the fields and uses a footpath down through the wood to the stream and up to Parsonage Farm, and through the yard to a small partly infilled quarry and a finger post **C**. Here you have two choices, either to the right to go to Tarr Steps and along the river to Withypool, or to the left to Withypool by the more direct route over Withypool Hill. Unless the Barle is in spate and Tarr Steps are impassable, or you are in a hurry, the Tarr Steps route, which takes you along the meandering Barle, is recommended. The description of the Withypool Hill route begins on p.112.

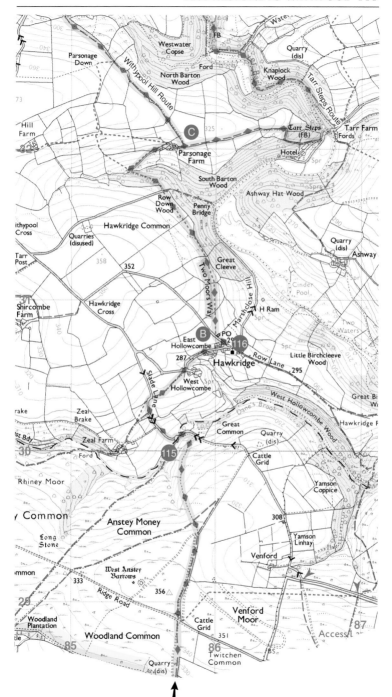

TARR STEPS ROUTE

If you are aiming for Tarr Steps walk along the edge of the field until you take to the vehicle track at 90 degrees to the right, then go through South Barton Wood, with bluebells and invasive Rhododendron ponticum, with its poisonous leaves, poisonous wood and poisonous roots, and down behind the Tarr Steps Hotel.

Tarr Steps **117** is an enigma. It is, self-evidently, a clapper bridge, made of the local sandstone; but how old? The earliest documents that mention it are Tudor, but it is probably a couple of hundred years older. Some would have it as a prehistoric structure. However old it is, it is a well-known beauty spot with excellent refreshments available at Tarr Farm.

Below the farm the Way is upriver along the permissive path through the field. The woods here are a SSSI. The main scientific interest is the lichens but most people will probably enjoy the variety of birds they can hear and which they might see. There are wood warblers among the trees, pied flycatchers in the canopy, redstarts on the fringes, and kingfishers, dippers and wagtails on the river. Dormice live in the hazel coppice and you might see the neatly gnawed, empty nuts they leave behind.

The walk alongside the bank takes you past a heronry **118** on the opposite bank and eventually you join the road **D** above the floodplain and drop back down to Withypool. The inn shown on the map is the Royal Oak **119**, which contains many hunting trophies. Various parts of stags, foxes, and otters are on display, and local opinion would probably be happy to see hunt saboteurs added to the display. But the law being what it is the clientele have to content themselves with a pinboard and cuttings about people who disrupt their sport. If you want to go to Exford Youth Hostel, which is 2¾ miles (4.5 km) away, take the permissive path to Exford which leaves the road 100 yards down the hill from **D**: go up the steps **E** into the wood and follow the yellow rectangles and arrows and then the path's continuation as a bridleway to Exford.

WITHYPOOL HILL ROUTE

From the partially infilled quarry and fingerpost **C** by Parsonage Farm head north-west along the bridlepath marked by blue arrows and blue blotches to reach the stream **E** near Westwater Farm. Go through the gate and turn right onto the road. This takes you past the farm and skirts Withypool Hill, with its Bronze Age stone circle, and down into Withypool. Go over the bridge and continue to the Royal Oak **119**.

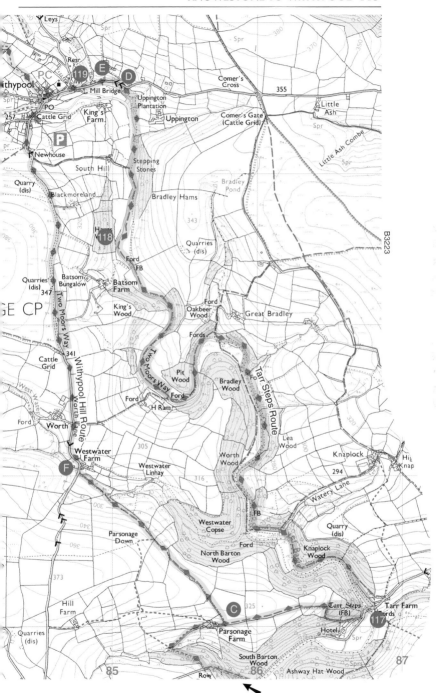

Leys
Resr
thypool
PC
119
E
D
Mill Bridge
Uppington Plantation
Uppington
PO
King's Farm
Cattle Grid
257
P
Newhouse
South Hill
Stepping Stones
Quarry (dis)
Blackmoreland
Hams
118
Ford
FB
Quarries (dis)
347
Batsom Bungalow
Batsom Farm
GE CP
Two Moors Way
King's Wood
Bradley Hams
343
Quarries (dis)
Bradley Pond
Comer's Cross
355
Little Ash
Comer's Gate (Cattle Grid)
Little Ash Combe
B3223
Ford
Oakbeer Wood
Great Bradley
Fords
341
Cattle Grid
Pit Wood
Two Moors Way
Ford
Bradley Wood
Tarr Steps Route
Ford
H Ram
Worth
305
Westwater Farm
F
Westwater Linhay
316
Worth Wood
Lea Wood
Knaplock
294
Hi Knap
Watery Lane
Withypool Hill Route
North Lane
West Water
Ford
300
340
Parsonage Down
360
Westwater Copse
FB
Quarry (dis)
Knaplock Wood
Hill Farm
373
Ford
North Barton Wood
325
C
Parsonage Farm
Tarr Steps (FB)
Tarr Farm
Fords
117
Hotel
Quarries (dis)
85
South Barton Wood
86
Ashway Hat Wood
87
Row

6 WITHYPOOL TO LYNMOUTH

via Exe Head   *16 miles (26 km)*

This section makes for a long day, and you may wish to have a shorter final section by staying in Simonsbath. There is an alternative route via Simonsbath, as well as a short alternative that cuts out some road walking. The latter initially uses the route towards Simonsbath. All routes meet at Exe Head on the open moor, and from there it is downhill nearly all the way to Lynmouth.

From the Royal Oak **119** you continue past the church and then bear right along the cul-de-sac. Just below is the post office stores, and the village telephone and public conveniences. From this road take the next right up the hill onto a path beside the old village school, and after four fields you are back on a road, Kitridge Lane. Turn left and after quite a length of beech hedges, during which time you can study the effects of different hedge-management regimes in

Sherdon Water flows through a typical steep-sided combe to the River Barle.

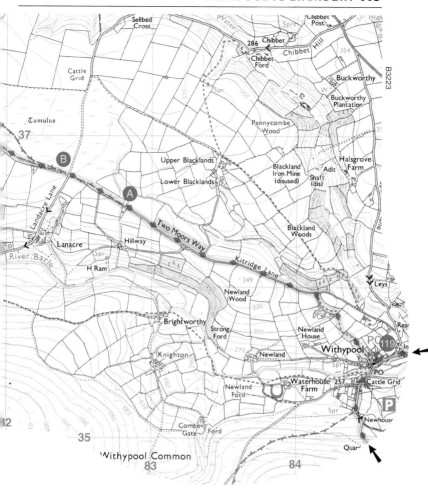

what is essentially a monoculture, you come to the end of the tarmac road. Through the gate **A** is moorland but this is not access land so you must follow the track, crossing Landacre ('Lan'acre') Lane **B** towards Simonsbath ('Simmunsbath'). Landacre Lane leads to the left to Landacre Bridge and to the right to Chibbet Cross, and on to Exford. There is a story that 'chibbet' is derived from gibbet as criminals were left to hang in chains as part of a former penal education programme. The penalty for taking one of the king's deer from the Forest was loss of a member, or death.

At the first fork take the left-hand track for Picked Stones, not the right for Gipsy Lane.

Wintershead Farm was built by the Knights in the 1840s. The farm buildings have a new lease of life as holiday accommodation.

At the second fork bear right; there may be a blue bridleway marker on the track that cuts through the nearby low bank: in 1996 you could see the marker by looking back once you were through the bank. The next fork offers the walker and rider the choice of route to Simonsbath, either via Cow Castle, to the left, or via Picked Stones, to the right. Bear left and after some moorland walking the track drops down through two gates and through a plantation above the Barle.

When the track finally reaches the crossing point of the Barle **C**, you have a choice of routes, depending on whether you wish to go via Cornham or via the village of Simonsbath. There is also a route that starts on the Simonsbath route then goes across access land to join the Cornham route: you can follow this route by using the appropriate descriptions and maps. The routes join at Exe Head. The description of the route via Simonsbath begins on p.122.

ROUTE VIA CORNHAM

Cross at the ford or by the bridge, waymarked to Blue Gate. The wooden superstructure of the bridge is bolted onto two railway lines, and this combination of flexibility and stiffness presumably explains the unexpected response to walkers crossing the structure. A smaller bridge over a tributary gets you back to the track from the ford up the combe. Further on in 1996 an automatic closer, a strip of inner tube from a tyre, was in use on a gate; a sad comment on walkers and riders. The chunks of white quartz lying on the grey slates in the stream bed show occasional traces of copper and iron, but there is no tin here, unlike Dartmoor.

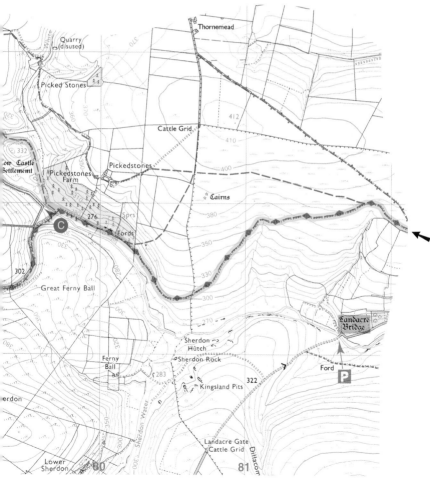

In fact there was not much of any metals. By Horsen Farm **120** the Way picks up a tarmac lane again, and the track you have just come up was waymarked as a R.U.P.P. in 1996, i.e. a road used as a public path. For those tempted to drive there is an older sign indicating 'track to Horsen Ford, unsuitable for cars'.

The new houses on the left, not yet on the map but visible for miles, were built for farm workers at Horsen Farm. The next farm, Wintershead Farm **121**, was built in the 1840s by Frederic Knight, who also built Horsen and several other Exmoor farms all in the same style as he continued his father's work of developing Exmoor. The farms were let on twenty-year leases with a low rent for the first four years. This attracted tenants but several came from areas of 'soft' farming and were ruined.

Walkers who kept on the path for Simonsbath but then crossed the bridge at Wheal Eliza

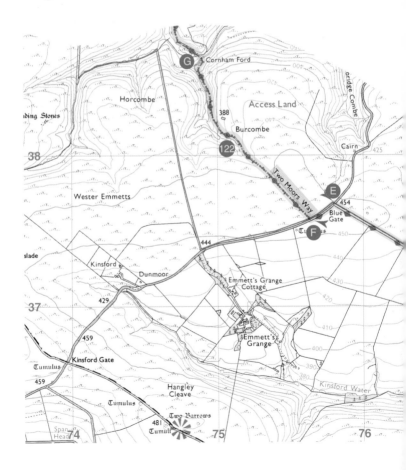

and came up over the access land might join the road at the gate near the corner **D**, or they might stay on the access land to come out at the road junction at Blue Gate **E**.

At the Blue Gate road junction **E**, turn left on the Simonsbath to South Molton road. A short way along, leave the road by the track on the right **F**, waymarked to 'Challacombe Road via Cornham Ford 1½ miles' over access land.

In places the green-grey slate has been permeated by haematite, red iron ore, and some pieces are noticeably heavy for their size. As the path steepens and the valley narrows **122** there are signs of attempts to find workable lodes of iron in this mineralized ground: channelled streams, pits, small quarries, dumps and even a length of iron tramway rail in the stream. Further down an east–west lode has been worked in a series of shallow pits that cross the valley. The mine was one of the Knight's ventures but it closed in 1856. The Dowlais Iron Company, which leased the mineral rights on the Knight's property, spent £6,000 in mining £650 worth of ore. There is no record of the results of the attempts to restart the mine in 1910.

At the mouth of the valley the brook cascades over moss to join a bigger stream that is crossed by a wooden bridge. Rejoin the track by the Cornham Ford **G** slightly down stream and as you go up the rocky defile there is an adit up to your right. This has been driven only a few feet, but it might be useful for shelter.

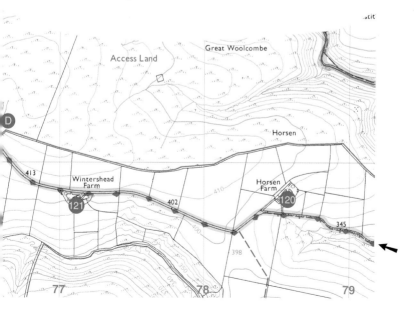

On Exe Head you may well see red deer rather than just more cross-bred ponies . . . but you will not get so close to the deer!

Beside the gate, where the Way leaves access land, is a winter-feeding pen for cattle. The hay or silage is put inside the central enclosure, and the cattle put their heads through the bars to eat, wearing away the galvanizing in the process. All the slurry drains down into the ditch behind the hedge. Cornham Farm is another farm built by the Knights, but the strange structure **123** in the field may arouse your curiosity. Was it for training the local tug-of-war team or stringing up a bullock for butchery? Smaller similar structures are used for camels in Libya. A pint of local cider might spur the imagination. At the end of Cornham Farm drive is the B3358 **H**. To the right are the Exmoor Foxhound Kennels and Simonsbath.

An earlier version of the Two Moors Way went left here but the present route avoids a road walk and crosses straight over and through the gate. The next gate is to the north-east and from there the path is marked by yellow-topped posts though you might need binoculars to see each successive one. Binoculars could also prove useful as red deer often lie up near the head of Tangs Bottom **124**. Continue through the gate onto the access land where you can walk up beside the wall to join the bridlepath from Pinkery Pond and the Tarka Trail, and go through the gate **I**. Pinkery is sometimes spelt Pinkworthy, but always pronounced 'Pinkery'. The pond was made by damming the infant River Barle. Why John Knight had his gangs of Irish labourers do this is an puzzle. Was it to hold water for powering mining machinery? For irrigation? To beautify his estate? The family papers are silent.

The Tarka Trail is a 180-mile (290-km) figure of eight, based on locations mentioned in Henry Williamson's book *Tarka the Otter*. The trail uses the Two Moors Way route to Lynmouth before taking the South West Coast Path, a National Trail, to Barnstaple.

A short distance down the path is the gate **J** by Exe Head, where the Simonsbath route joins.

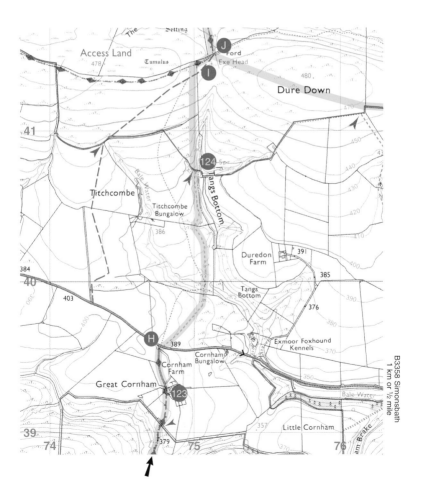

ROUTE VIA SIMONSBATH.

Continue up the path around the east side of Cow Castle **125**. This hill fort probably dates from about 500 BC. 'Cow' is thought to have been derived from the Celtic 'caer'. As you walk up the path you will come to a footbridge **K**. The path to Simonsbath does not cross the bridge but if you want to go via Cornham you should cross onto land owned by the National Park and head up the tracks, keeping the tree enclosure **L** on your left. The NNE–SSW fence you can cross at several places and then leave the access land by the bend in the road **D** or else at Blue Gate **E**. The National Park's management aims to introduce heather here rather than having predominantly purple moor grass. Farmers like the grass because, after burning, its new growth gives a good early bite for stock. Very few other plants can survive an annual burn, so ecologically the land becomes rather uninteresting.

If you wish to continue to Simonsbath you carry on walking past evidence of mining. Some of this is possibly 16th-century trials, but the Knights also opened Wheal Eliza here as a copper mine in 1846, though it closed as an iron mine in 1854. The ore had 1 per cent copper and 60 per cent iron. The entrepreneurial Knights used Cornish miners, which is why the Cornish word for mine, wheal, is used.

The summits of Flexbarrow **126** and Cow Castle are at approximately the same height and are probably relics of an old river terrace, formed as the Barle incised its meanders into the slaty rock.

The path now continues along near the river then enters Birch Cleave **127**, a steep-sided hill (a cleave) now covered with over-mature beeches. These trees were planted before 1840 and there is some suggestion that this was a tree nursery. The National Park owns the wood and is trying to encourage natural regrowth.

Take care when you come out on the road **M**. Cross over and turn right up the hill, past the Exmoor Forest Hotel, and take the road on the left to the public conveniences and the terraced car park at the bottom of Ashcombe. From the upper car park take the footpath to Preyway Head. The local fox hunt usually draws this wood **128** so you just might see a fox.

At the top of the wood you cross the stile and continue up Ashcombe, following the yellow-topped posts to a gate. Follow the leat to the left for a short way, before going up to the gate **N** on the right of the stock-handling pens. Once over this gate you are in a field and on access land and you need to head a few degrees north of west to reach the gate at Preyway Head **O**. There is no exit further up the hill.

Walk up the road to the car park, a disused piece of road, and through the gate **P** towards Dure Down. There is a path through the first field and then after the gate keep to the wall on your left until you go through another gate **Q**. From here walk roughly north-west to Exe Head. Some

Birch Cleave no longer has birches but many weedy beeches. Possibly it was originally a beech nursery.

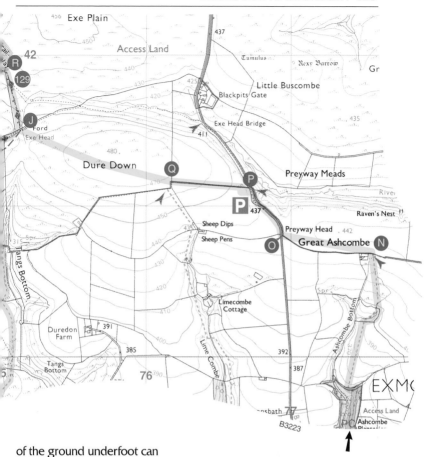

of the ground underfoot can
be soft. Hares live here and you may well
also see deer. On a sunny summer's day the air can be full of the
sound of skylarks, and you might also see a merlin hunting them. At
the gate **J** at Exe Head the Simonsbath route joins the Cornham route.

Go through the gate, taking the path to Hoar Oak. By the gate is a
tiny trickle that you ford with no difficulty: this is the Exe, flowing to
the English Channel, and after you cross the saddle **129** all the land
ahead drains to the Bristol Channel. Reaching this watershed is more
of an achievement for those walking from Ivybridge!

The Way takes the track downhill **R** through the low earth-bank,
and follows the stream. It may be the merest trickle by the bank but
within a hundred yards enough water has seeped out of the spongy
peat for the stream to produce a range of gurgling, murmuring and
splashing sounds suitable for a young stream.

At the bottom the Way fords both streams and follows the left side of Hoar Oak Water. Above the track is a ruined sheepfold **130** with a room for the shepherd on the east side, looking out over the valley. There may be other details here but stones have been moved about irresponsibly recently making the layout harder to interpret. The sheepfold dates from before the 1840s when Frederic Knight enclosed the Hoar Oak Herding, certainly very recently compared to the Bronze Age Erme Pound near the other end of the Two Moors Way, with maybe a 4,500 years history.

Above a line of beeches the track comes to a gate in a bank, but the Way goes steeply down to the stream without crossing the bank. The route is then through the gate in the bank on the other side of the stream. The tree by the gate is the Hoar Oak Tree **131**, now fenced in with a strand of barbed wire on top of the fence for good measure. Earlier there was a railing around the tree but the sheep's feet were eroding the soil and damaging the roots. The 'Hore Oke' is on Speed's map of 1610. That tree fell in 1658, though the records of a hoar oak here go back to the 13th century. The next tree lasted from 1662 to 1916. The latest Hoar Oak is the survivor of a dozen planted in 1917, and its slow growth is mocked by the robust rowan nearby. The healthy beeches were probably planted after Frederic Knight had enclosed Hoar Oak Herding in the 1840s when his tenants were allowed reduced rents for planting hedgebanks. The wall is the boundary of the Forest of Exmoor, and also the boundary between Devon and Somerset.

Once through the gate, head gently uphill on the track initially going approximately north-north-east. The thin green doughnut across the valley is another sheepfold **132**, made in a similar fashion to Iron Age earthworks by cutting a circular ditch and throwing the earth inwards. This particular earthwork probably dates from the 1870s when Frederic Knight brought northern English and Scottish shepherds to the area and they built these 'pinfolds' or 'stells' in their own style.

The Way joins a track that turns into a turf track with heather on either side. The cairn **133** is not much, just a few short upright stones and some debris.

By now the Way is almost a ridge walk, though the ridge is more a plateau sloping gently in all directions rather than a crest. There is another parallel track a few yards to the east with slightly better views to the east. To the north on a clear day Wales is visible. As you come down Cheriton Ridge there is a good view of the steep-sided wooded valley of the Hoar Oak Water and further to the right on the skyline the building with the mast is the television relay station on Countisbury Hill. Most of the equipment is inside the old coastguard look-out.

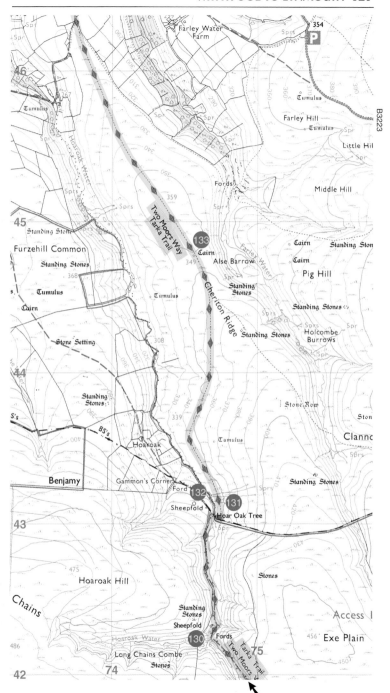

Looking up a placid Hoar Oak Water onto the Forest of Exmoor.

The final few miles of the Two Moors Way.

As you leave the Moor there is a waymarker stating 'Two Moors Way' and pointing south, and 'Two Moors Way, Cheriton' to the north. Walk down the rough lane to the tarmac road **S**, where the Way now turns left (an older route went right) to Scoresdown. After Scoresdown the Way continues down a track to cross the river, the Hoar Oak Water, at Smallcombe Bridge. Turn right through the gate onto the permissive path through the NT's Combe Park **134** property. These woods are part of the Watersmeet SSSI, designated to protect the wide range of habitats within one of the largest semi-natural woodlands in south-west England.

Sessile oak dominates the woods. Near the gate there is an under storey of hazel, ash, rowan and holly and a tasty ground cover includes whortleberries (though bye-laws prohibit anyone from removing anything from NT land). Areas with a bare floor are favoured by wood warblers, a characteristic bird of western sessile oak woods. The river sides are covered in places by a thicket of Japanese Knotweed, which is certainly not protected. The plant was introduced to beautify gardens and has now become an invasive pest, which many, including the NT, spend a lot of time, money and ingenuity trying to control. Various rare butterflies are also found in the SSSI and efforts are made by the NT to improve the breeding success of the High Brown Fritillary.

At the hotel's riverside games field the Way bears off left way-marked to 'Watersmeet & NT Car Park'. Then go sharply right over a stile behind the hotel's garden wall. Just beyond the octagonal stone summer-house and down some steps the Way goes right, over a stile to Watersmeet, rather than straight on up to the NT car park.

The Way is then again beside the river, and passes beneath several specimen conifers, including a Douglas fir and a larch, and then another Douglas fir before the NT car park above Hillsford Bridge.

At the main road **T**, the A39 Barnstaple to Lynmouth road, walk up the road to the next hairpin bend. On the right side there is a grass verge to walk on for most of the way, though for a short distance you walk on the road side of the crash barrier. In summer you will proba-bly be happy when you reach the bend and the track **U** waymarked to Lynmouth through the NT's Watersmeet Estate.

At the top of the climb the path cuts through Myrtleberry South Camp **135**, an Iron Age hill-fort, then keeps close to the contour line before climbing again to continue always towards Lynmouth, with spectacular views over the deep wooded valleys. Myrtleberry is another name for whortleberry.

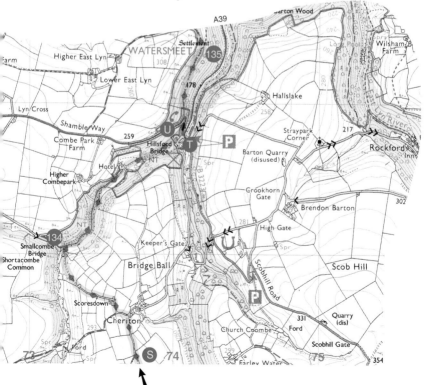

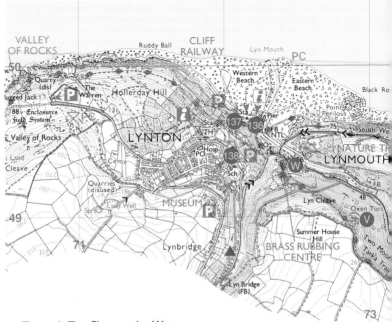

Through The Cleeves the Way
has some steep climbs and descents, made easier
by carefully made zigzag paths. If you thought it was all downhill for
walkers from the watershed at Exe Head this will have surprised you.

At Oxen Tor **V** those who wish to go to Lynton Youth Hostel can
bear left while the Way branches downhill to the right. Once past the
metal NT sign at the edge of the Watersmeet Estate you keep straight
on at the next junction. The final few steps before the houses of
Lynmouth may be dark and dismal but that's a trifling amount to pay
for all the splendours of the previous 89 miles (143 km).

The final granite Two Moors Way marker **W** is where the alley
meets the road, beside the Bonnicott Hotel, and the Two Moors Way
currently ends without any fuss in the car park down the street where
the buses stop. Information about the services from here, and how to
get the up-to-date timetable, is in the final section of this book enti-
tled 'Useful Information'.

If you want to spend some time exploring Lynmouth and its twin,
Lynton, the best way is to start with the Exmoor National Park Visitor
Centre **136**, the only bright spot in the rather sad seaside pavilion. If you
have completed the Way there is a book in the centre you can sign if you
so wish. Alongside the pavilion are the limekilns in which limestone
from South Wales was burnt with culm, the local name for anthracite

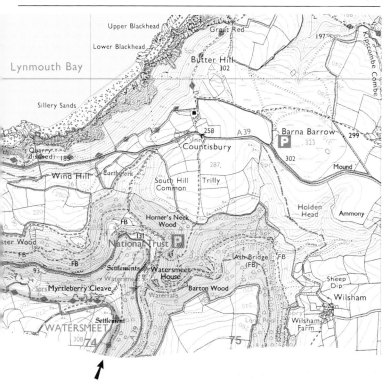

dust, which was brought over with the limestone. Culm is also the name for the very poor sooty coals found in a few seams in the rocks further south, the Culm Measures, over which much of the central section of the Way ran. The lime from the kilns was spread on the sour fields to sweeten them so crops grew better. Beyond the kilns is the cliff railway **137** to Lynton. This simple system uses the weight of a tank full of water in the descending car to pull the ascending car up. Who needs complexity? The buildings in Lynton, like those in Lynmouth, are of no great age, but there is a helpful TIC and the Lyn and Exmoor Museum **138** and further up the valley in Lynbridge is the youth hostel. Between the three communities you should be able to find most of the shops and facilities you might need: post office, bank and a range of shops, including one selling outdoor gear. And as a reminder of what the weather in this part of the world can do, you will see many references to the disaster of August 1952. Nine inches of rain fell in twenty-four hours on The Chains and caused a massive surge of water, boulders and trees down the rivers. Most of the buildings around the harbour were destroyed and twenty-eight people died.

USEFUL
INFORMATION

TRANSPORT

You can reach Ivybridge and Lynmouth, at the two ends of the Two Moors Way, quite easily by public transport, but because this part of the world relies heavily on tourism doing so is easier in summer than in winter. Trains from Ivybridge connect with long-distance services at Exeter and Plymouth. From Lynmouth you need to catch a bus to Barnstaple to connect with trains on the 'Tarka Line' to Exeter. Alternatively, between June and September, you can take the bus all the way to Exeter from Lynmouth, either enjoying the views on the coastal link to Minehead then on to Exeter, or going via Dulverton to Exeter. In summer there is also the option of steaming along the West Somerset Railway for 20 miles from Minehead to Bishops Lydeard, with a bus link through to Taunton railway station.

Long-distance coach services, run by National Express, will take you to Exeter, Plymouth, Ilfracombe, Barnstaple, and in summer to Minehead. There are direct services from London and Birmingham to Barnstaple, and from many places to Exeter and Plymouth, but from some starting points you may need to change coaches at London Heathrow, Birmingham or Bristol.

Those walking only part of the Two Moors Way might wish to use Morchard Road station on the Tarka Line, or catch a bus in a village on or close to the Way. In Summer 1996 the following places had bus services: Ivybridge, Holne, New Bridge, Widecombe-in-the-Moor, Warren House Inn, Chagford, Drewsteignton, Hittisleigh, Colebrooke, Coleford, Morchard Road, Morchard Bishop, Black Dog, Witheridge, Knowstone, East Anstey, Tarr Steps, Withypool, Simonsbath, Watersmeet and Lynmouth. In winter this list effectively shrinks to Ivybridge, Chagford, Drewsteignton, Coleford, Morchard Road, Black Dog, Witheridge and Lynmouth as the other places have little or no bus service. In rural areas buses will stop anywhere safe on request. There may be only one bus a week, or several a day, so you will need to have a public transport map and the public transport guides, which are available free for the whole of the relevant area from the Transport Co-ordination Centre, Environment Department, County Hall, Exeter, EX2 4QW.

Finally, Brittany Ferries' ships come into Plymouth from Brittany (Roscoff) and Spain (Santander), and British Airways flies into Plymouth from London Heathrow and Cork.

Telephone enquiry lines:
National Rail Enquiries on 0345 484950. This is available 7 days a week 24 hours a day. Telesales for tickets, with or without reservations, is on 0171 313 1950 and is available Monday to Friday 8.00a.m. to 8.00p.m. and on Saturday from 9.00a.m. to 5.00p.m. The tickets will be sent to you.
National Express on 0990 808080. Open 7 days a week, 8.00 a.m. to 10.00 p.m. You can buy tickets with reservations, paying by credit card, and have them sent to you.
Public transport information in Devon on Plymouth (01752), Exeter (01392), Barnstaple (01271) or Torquay (01803) 382800. Open Monday to Friday, 9.00 a.m. to 5.00 p.m..
Public transport information in Somerset on 01823 358299. Open Monday to Friday, 8.00 a.m. to 5.00 p.m..
West Somerset Railway on 01643 704996 (general enquiries) or 01643 707650 (talking timetable).
Brittany Ferries on 0990 360360.
British Airways on 0345 222111.

Accommodation

There is a good range of accommodation along the Two Moors Way: camp sites, camping barns, youth hostels, bed-and-breakfast places (often in farmhouses), pubs and hotels. The development of a network of camping barns is being very actively promoted, both for the benefit of walkers and to provide a use for otherwise redundant farm-buildings. As for youth hostels, there are three on or close to the Way – Bellever, Exford and Lynton – while Plymouth or Exeter might be useful before starting at Ivybridge.

Accommodation for the Two Moors Way is listed in Stilwell's *National Trail Companion*, which is updated annually. Accommodation lists can also be obtained from the Two Moors Way Association by post, or from Ivybridge TIC, Lynton TIC and the Exmoor National Park Visitor Centre at Lynmouth. To receive the latest list by post send fifty pence in stamps plus a stamped addressed envelope, or two international postal reply coupons, to Joe Turner, Honorary Secretary TMWA, Coppins, The Poplars, Pinhoe, Exeter, EX4 9HH. In summer walkers are advised to book, and booking early should minimize unwanted diversions off route.

Information about youth hostels is in the annual *YHA Accommodation Guide*, published by the Youth Hostels Association, 8 St Stephen's Hill, St Albans, AL1 2DY. Tel. 01727 855215. If you are not already a member of a hostelling association affiliated to the IYHF, you can join the YHA at any hostel. There is no upper age limit in Britain.

You can obtain the latest information about camping barns from the YHA camping barns booking office at North Devon Holiday Homes, 19 Cross Street, Barnstaple, EX31 1BD. Tel. 01271 24420. Holne, the original camping barn, can only be booked direct on 01364 643920. By early 1997 there will be six camping barns convenient for the Way. Users do not need to be members of the YHA, but do need to bring at least a sleeping bag, and, for most of the camping barns, all their camping equipment except a tent.

Backpackers may camp on unenclosed moorland on Dartmoor, subject to a commonsense code. You are not likely to fall foul of local bye-laws if you are at least 100 metres from any road, not visible from roads and houses, and not in a reservoir catchment area or on one of the very small commons heavily used for recreation, and do not use a pitch for more than two nights. Do put your camping stove on a rock, and light no other fires. Take all your litter out with you, and bury human excrement: no one wants the Two Moors Way to become another 'kleenex trail'. Considerate campers leave their pitches as they would wish to find them, and sadly this occasionally means having to carry out someone else's litter.

INFORMATION AND VISITOR CENTRES

Tourist Information Centres provide information about the local area, and the rest of Britain. Those at the ends of the Two Moors Way are: Ivybridge South Dartmoor TIC, Leonard's Road, Ivybridge. Tel. 01752 897035. Lynton TIC, Town Hall, Lynton. Tel. 01598 752225.

In addition there is a TIC at Exeter Services, at Junction 30 on the M5, and another on the A374 to Plymouth, off the A38 at the Marsh Mills fly-over on the edge of Plymouth.

Both National Park centres on the Way are seasonal:

Exmoor National Park Visitor Centre, The Esplanade, Lynmouth. Tel. 01598 752509.

Dartmoor National Park Information Centre is in a caravan at New Bridge. Tel. 01364 631303.

In both National Parks you will find information points in villages. In 1996 those on, or close to, the Way were in Holne (Post Office), Chagford (Old Forge Tea Rooms), Widecombe-in-the-Moor (Sexton's Cottage, owned by the National Trust), and Withypool (Post Office and Stores).

WEATHER FORECASTS

You can hear Meteorological Office Weathercall forecasts on 0891 500404 for Devon and Cornwall and on 0891 500405 for Somerset. The corresponding marine forecasts, Marinecall, are on 0891 500458 and 0891 500549.

USEFUL ADDRESSES

Dartmoor National Park Authority, Parke, Haytor Road, Bovey Tracey, Devon, TQ13 9JQ. Tel. 01626 832093. DNPA publishes a free annual newspaper, *Dartmoor Visitor*, plus a range of leaflets and documents which are widely available and can also be obtained by post.

Exmoor National Park Authority, Exmoor House, Dulverton, Somerset, TA22 9HL. Tel. 01398 323665. ENPA publishes a free annual newspaper, *Exmoor Visitor*, plus a range of leaflets and documents that are widely available and can also be obtained by post.

English Heritage, 429 Oxford Street, London, W1R 2HD. Tel. 0171 973 3434.

English Nature, Devon, Cornwall & Isles of Scilly Team, The Old Mill House, 37 North Street, Okehampton, EX20 1AR. Tel. 01837 55045. English Nature, Somerset Team, Roughmoor, Bishop's Hull, Taunton, TA1 5AA. Tel. 01823 283211.

Environment Agency, SW Region, Manley House, Kestrel Way, Exeter, EX2 7LQ. Tel. 01392 444000. The official environmental protection agency, incorporating the old National Rivers Authority. 0800 80 70 60, the emergency hotline for reporting all environmental incidents relating to air, land and water, is available twenty-four hours a day.

Forest Enterprise, Peninsula Forest District, Bullers Hill, Kennford, Exeter, EX6 7XR. Tel. 01392 832262. Forest Enterprise is a part of the Forestry Commission.

Ordnance Survey, Romsey Road, Maybush, Southampton, SO16 4GU. Tel. 01703 792000.

The following voluntary organizations all play a part in conserving what you will see, hear and touch on the Two Moors Way. You may feel like supporting them.

Dartmoor Preservation Association, Freepost, Plymouth, PL1 1BR.

Dartmoor Rescue Group, General Secretary: John Whiting, Bratton, Rectory Road, Bridestowe, Okehampton, EX20 4ER. If the rescue group's services are needed you must make contact through the police.

Devon Wildlife Trust, 35-37 St David's Hill, Exeter, EX4 4DA. Tel. 01392 279244.

Exmoor Search and Rescue Team, Chairman: John Wright, Barnfield House, Bishop's Tawton, Barnstaple, EX32 0BG. If the search and rescue team's services are needed you must make contact through the police.

Exmoor Society, Parish Rooms, Dulverton, TA22 9DP.

Friends of National Parks, Freepost, London, SW11 1BR.

Landmark Trust, Shottesbrooke, Maidenhead, SL6 3SW. Tel. 01628 825920. The Trust rents out three properties at Lettaford, including Sanders, one of the best longhouses.

National Trust, Devon office: Killerton House, Broadclyst, Exeter, EX5 3LE. Tel. 01392 881691. Somerset is in the Wessex region: Eastleigh Court, Bishopstrow, Warminster, BA12 9HW. Tel. 01985 843600.

Ramblers' Association, 1-5 Wandsworth Road, London, SW8 2XX. Tel. 0171 5826878.

Royal Society for the Protection of Birds, South West Office, 10 Richmond Road, Exeter, EX4 4JA. Tel. 01392 432691.

Somerset Wildlife Trust, Fyne Court, Broomfield, Bridgewater, TA5 2EQ. Tel. 01823 451587.

Woodland Trust, Autumn Park, Dysart Road, Grantham, NG31 6LL. Tel. 01476 574297.

Rangers

Both National Parks have uniformed rangers, each with their own area. If you need to contact a ranger during office hours please call the headquarters of the relevant park authority. On Dartmoor at weekends between 10.00 a.m. and 4.00 p.m. you should call the High Moorland Visitor Centre at Princetown (01822 890414). Outside these hours if you need to contact a ranger urgently you will either need to use the phone number of the relevant ranger (published each year in the *Dartmoor Visitor* and *Exmoor Visitor*) or call the police.

Events and guided walks

In both National Parks there are excellent programmes of guided walks, gentle education about many aspects of the moors. The walks are listed in the free newspapers, with an indication as to whether they are designed for the casual walker or for those interested in more strenuous events.

Guided walks, and other events, are also organized in the area by the Devon Wildlife Trust, Forest Enterprise and the National Trust.

There are many leaflets detailing local self-guided walks, which are available either free or costing at most one pound. Publishers include both National Park Authorities, the Tarka Project, the National Trust, and Forest Enterprise as well as the following local authorities:

South Hams District Council, Follaton House, Plymouth Road, Totnes, TQ9 5NE. Tel. 01803 861234. There is a guided walk programme too.

Teignbridge District Council, Forde House, Newton Abbot, TQ12 4XX. Tel. 01626 61101.

West Devon Borough Council, Kilworthy Park, Drake Road, Tavistock, PL19 0BZ. Tel. 01822 615911. Guided walks too.

Mid Devon District Council, 1 Westexe South, Tiverton, EX16 5DQ. Tel. 01884 255718.

The free public transport timetables for Dartmoor and Exmoor also include self-guided walks.

ORDNANCE SURVEY MAPS COVERING THE TWO MOORS WAY

Landranger (1:50 000)
202, 191, 181, 180.
Touring Map & Guide (1:63 360)
1 (Dartmoor) and 5 (Exmoor – map only).
For complete coverage at 1:25 000 you will need 8 maps:
Outdoor Leisure (1:25 000): 28 (Dartmoor) and 9 (Exmoor).
Pathfinder (1:25 000): 1294, 1313, 1256, 1275, 1276, 1295.

BIBLIOGRAPHY

Beacham, Peter, (ed.), *Devon Building*, Devon Books, 1990.

Binding, H., (ed.), *Exmoor – 40 years on*, Exmoor Books, 1994.

Binding, H., (ed.), *The Changing Face of Exmoor*, Exmoor Books, 1995.

Blackmore, R.D., *Lorna Doone*, Nelson, 1869, Penguin, 1994.

Bourne, H., *Living on Exmoor*, The Galley Press, 1963, Exmoor Books, 1991.

Brewer, Dave, *A Field Guide to the Boundary Markers on and around Dartmoor*, Devon Books, 1986.

Burton, S.H., *Exmoor*, Robert Hale, 1969 & 1984.

Butler, Jeremy, *Dartmoor Atlas of Antiquities, Volume One, The East*, Devon Books, 1991.

Butler, Jeremy, *Dartmoor Atlas of Antiquities, Volume Four, The South-East*, Devon Books, 1993.

Crossing, William, *Guide to Dartmoor*, Western Morning News, 1909, republished by Peninsula Press, 1990.

Crossing, William, *Crossing's Dartmoor Worker*, 1903, republished by Peninsula Press, 1990.

Greeves, Tom, *The Archaeology of Dartmoor from the Air*, Devon Books, 1985.

Greeves, Tom, *Tin Mines and Miners of Dartmoor: A Pictorial Record*, Devon Books, 1986.

Grinsell, L.V., *The Archaeology of Exmoor*, David & Charles, 1970.

Harris, Helen, *The Industrial Archaeology of Dartmoor*, David & Charles, 1968, Peninsula Press, 1992.

Hemery, E., *High Dartmoor: Land and People*, Robert Hale, 1983.

Hoskins, W.G., *Devon*, David & Charles, 1954, Devon Books, 1992.

Mabey, Richard, *Food for Free*, Collins, 1972 & 1989.

Perkins, John W., *Geology Explained: Dartmoor and the Tamar Valley*, David & Charles, 1974.

Pevsner, N., and revised by same and Bridget Cherry, *Devon – The Buildings of England*, Penguin, 1952 and 1989.

Pevsner, N., (ed.), *South and West Somerset – The Buildings of England*, Penguin, 1958.

Phillpotts, Eden, *Widecombe Fair*, John Murray, 1913, Mott, 1983.

Polling, E.J., *The Exmoor Pony*, The Exmoor Pony Society, 1986.

Sitters, H.P., (ed.), *Tetrad Atlas of the Breeding Birds of Devon*, Devon Bird Watching and Preservation Society, 1988.

Stilwell, Tim & Conway, Dean (eds.), *National Trail Companion*, Stilwell, 1996.

Weir, John, (ed.), *Dartmoor National Park*, Webb & Bower/Michael Joseph/Countryside Commission, 1987.

Williamson, Henry, *Tarka the Otter*, Putnam 1927, Penguin 1971.

Woods, Stephen H., *Dartmoor Stone*, Devon Books, 1988.

Worth, R. Hansford, *Dartmoor*, 1953, republished as *Worth's Dartmoor* by Peninsula Press, 1967.

PLACES TO VISIT NEAR THE TWO MOORS WAY

Suggestions about places to visit on the Two Moors Way are mentioned in the route descriptions: places to visit that can be reached by public transport are listed below. You are advised to check for opening hours, especially out of season.

High Moorland Visitor Centre, Princetown. Tel. 01822 890414. This is the main visitor centre for Dartmoor, and is open every day except Christmas Day and Boxing Day.

Exmoor National Park Visitor Centre at Dulverton. Tel. 01398 323841. This is open all year, but with restricted opening in winter.

Crediton. Birthplace of St Boniface in about 680, patron saint of Germany, Crediton was a bishopric before the see was transferred to Exeter in 1050. Fine church, and one mile long main street with many Georgian and early Victorian buildings. Town trail leaflet available from TIC.

Dartmoor Prison Museum, Princetown. Tel. 01822 890261. 'Opening depends on operational requirements'.

Exeter. Despite air-raids and post-war town-planners, Exeter still has an amazing wealth for the visitor, including Roman walls, the cathedral begun by the Normans, Guildhall, Customs House and canal basin, merchants' houses, and the main museum and art gallery of Devon. There is a youth hostel.

Finch Foundry, Sticklepath, on the old A30 east of Okehampton. Tel. 01837 840046. A water-powered foundry making small hand-tools, and now owned by the National Trust. Marked on some maps as the 'Museum of Water Power'.

Lyn & Exmoor Museum, Market Street, Lynton. Tel. 01598 752317.

Museum of Dartmoor Life, West Street, Okehampton. Tel. 01837 52295. Self-guided walk to Finch Foundry.

Museum of North Devon, The Square, Barnstaple. Tel. 01271 46747. A good local museum.

Okehampton Castle. Tel. 01837 52844. Originally a round Norman keep, the ruin is owned by English Heritage.

Plymouth. The largest city in Devon, Plymouth has a good museum, and evidence of centuries of naval and mercantile history, which is becoming more accessible to visitors as the Royal Navy's needs decrease.

BROKEN WAYMARKS, BOARDWALKS, KISSING GATES, BRIDGES OR STILES

Please help other walkers and farmers by reporting any damage to Devon County Environment Department, Lucombe House, County Hall, Exeter, EX2 4QW. Tel. 01392 382249. Please give the grid reference and a description of the location as well as the nature of the problem: the information will be forwarded to the relevant person.